COURAGEOUS
CHURCHES

COURAGEOUS
CHURCHES

Refusing Decline
Inviting Growth

PAUL T. HEINECKE
KENT R. HUNTER
DAVID S. LUECKE

Publishing House
St. Louis

Copyright © 1991 Concordia Publishing House
3558 S. Jefferson Avenue, St. Louis, MO 63118-3968
Manufactured in the United States of America

Library of Congress Cataloging-in-Publication Data

Heinecke, Paul T., 1921–
    Courageous churches : refusing decline, inviting growth / Paul T. Heinecke, Kent R. Hunter, David S. Luecke.
        p.   ˙cm.
    ISBN 0-570-04561-4
    1. Church growth—Lutheran Church—Missouri Synod. 2. Lutheran Church—Missouri Synod—Membership. 3. Lutheran Church—Membership. I. Hunter, Kent R., 1947– . II. Luecke, David S., 1940– . III. Title.
BX8061.M7H35   1992
284.1'322—dc20   91-23736

1 2 3 4 5 6 7 8 9 10 VP 00 99 98 97 96 95 94 93 92 91

Contents

CONTENTS

Foreword

The title *Courageous Churches,* put me off at first. Holding the manuscript in my hand it felt wrong—a kind of Madison Avenue affectation, selected for its buyer-attraction potential. Who ever heard of a courageous church? Courageous people? Yes. Churches? No one ever called one that in my memory.

As I read the manuscript my first impression moderated. The title selection started feeling better. I began to wonder whether the authors might have zeroed in on an essential but heretofore undiscovered key congregational quality. Possible? Possible.

Now, having read the book, I am convinced that the title is proper and accurate. Courage—plain, old-fashioned, unembellished courage—is one of the basic ingredients for developing dedicated, effective service by pastor and parish alike. The courage I read about is more than a synonym for some hard-to-define characteristic of authentic Christian congregational living. It is a distinct and precise *first* element in a sequence of serving that starts with courage, moves on to effectiveness, and concludes with success.

Success. Why does that word upset and/or scare pastors and congregations so much? My guess is that so many have functioned with so few victories for so long they've forgotten what winning is like. They are the 20th century twin of the man crippled for 38 years (John 5) who had become so adapted to his condition that he failed the easy answer to Jesus' targeting question, "Do you want to get well?" Many of us, too, have become so accustomed to low/no results that we believe success is abnormal! Success is suspect. Our patron saint is Philip.

Philip was the first to respond to Jesus' question on the day he fed the 5,000 (John 6:1–14). In the blink of an eye he began demonstrating his skill in the art of justifying failure. Remember? Christ had asked, "Where shall we buy bread for these people to eat?" Philip scowled, wrinkled his brow, and set to work with focused energy, developing a planning model for proving nothing could be done. How? He sensibly counted the people, multiplied their number by the amount of food each would require, figured the cost of that projected mountain of food, subtracted the bottom line from the balance sheet of Jesus, Inc., and came up with the only answer. It can't be done! What a relief!

This book is about people who came up with a different answer in similar circumstances. If *we-never-did-it-that-way-before* are the seven last words of dying churches, the antecedent is much simpler: *It-can't-be-done.* To which many of us attach a sanitizing P.S. *not if you use proper theological presuppositions.* That caveat guarantees "it" won't be done—and often leaves us with a triumphant feeling of theological loyalty to boot! The people this book reports on have received courage through their theological loyalty to develop how-to, not how-not-to. But I'm getting ahead of myself.

I don't know what Jesus said to Philip after his report. Maybe nothing. Maybe all He did was give His disciple a pained look. There had to be at least *that.* Whatever—Philip slides off stage center and disciple 2, Andrew, slips on. His is a slightly improved perception of task. Slightly. Ignoring the needs of the 5,000, Andrew downshifts. He probably decides that what Jesus *really* meant by his question was how do you feed 14: Jesus, 12 disciples, and (common decency demands no less) the young man whose mother had loaded him down with such a wonderfully enormous lunch that it just might be enough to do the job. No big and obviously impossible task of feeding a world of hungry people! Andrew adopted a more manageable objective of convincing a starry-eyed kid that sharing lunch with Jesus and His friends was a Godly activity that needed immediate implementation.

So much for the disciples' understanding of task. With that Jesus seems to have ignored them for further planning purposes. But not the boy. And not the lunch. Not the need of the original 5,000. Jesus took over and in the process modeled the kind of courage this book is all about.

It's interesting that the first thing He did was call for just a tad of modestly courageous response from his low-visioned followers. Just a little bit. He gave them an assignment: "Make them sit down." Anyone can do that, right? Well, maybe. I've spent most of a lifetime trying to get people to sit down and services started. It's not easy—

as any pastor will tell you. For the disciples the simple assignment was further complicated *because He didn't tell them what was coming next.* Sure, they could ask people to sit down, but who willingly sits down if they don't know why they should—and you can't tell them? Except maybe to limply say "He said so," like they were later told to say as they commandeered that Palm Sunday donkey. Following through on that order required courage. And courage was answered. The crowd sat down. They sat so everyone could see the miracle!

Having taken care of the sitting part, there developed a second problem. Think about it. How do you break bread and divide fish— for 5,000? How long does it take? And who is going to do *that.* And how do you distribute food to 5,000? All those tasks demand hard work. And they are only the first two steps. More hard work is coming. Courage, applied, is not for the lazy.

Who, but Jesus would think about policing the field afterward, picking up what fell to the ground? Twelve baskets of excess, just to prove the point. One for every disciple who thought it couldn't be done.

The point? This book is not only about courage and faith. It's also about hard work and about lots of people rolling up their sleeves to get important work for Christ completed. It's about how we ought deal with God's abundance . . . a problem few have because they are afraid to take the first steps of faithfulness that sets the stage for God's promised explosions of largess. They are low on courage. But the authors of this book aren't.

I have known the three hard-working authors of this book for many years. I hold them in admiration for many things, not the least of which is their ability to step back from doing congregational work in order to enter the serving world of teaching. To me that's courage *compounded.* Each has the right stuff for the parish and the pastoral ministry. That old saw, Those who can, do; and those who can't, teach, does not fit Hunter, Heinecke, and Luecke. They can each do. They can also teach. Through this book, as in the classroom, they seek students. Any volunteers?

In preparing *Courageous Churches,* the threesome not only worked hard but have done us a special favor. Beside packing these pages with the insights they have gathered and developed over the years, they have woven into their material great reportings of courage from 50 of the Christian world's finest doers. *Courageous* doers.

The world of courageous doers is not very large. I'm glad to report that it's larger than the 50 pastors/congregations reported herein. But it's not a whole lot larger. Compared to the tens of thousands of trained and certified pastors—and the equal thousands of congregations—only a handful of either seems to have absorbed the skills, developed the commitment and found the will to move into the realm of courageous action.

When I read the names of congregations and pastors from the courage list, I was not surprised. I have long known, or known of, most of the 50 ministries and pastoral leaders about whom this book gives report. Not all, though. Some of the parishes are new in the Christian community and have grown almost unnoticed. And some of the pastors are still quite young. One of them, Dennis Schiefelbein, has already gone home. He was a courageous pastoral comet who blazed briefly but so brightly against the night sky. Receiving his Lord's final commendation came far too early to my way of thinking. I pray our Lord will raise up a replacement. Soon. We need more like him.

What sets this book apart from others is the happy marriage between the authors and the subjects. They complement each other. Finishing the last page, your appetite for serving is whetted and the understanding of potential for service is expanded. In *Courageous Churches* one group of courageous servants provides the data for action and another gives order to their report. Between them they pack these pages with hundreds of ideas begging to be considered, adapted, and applied. And the ideas will be used—if thousands of parishes who have a yen to be courageous will let the creative serving-juices simmer to full boil. Just give them a chance.

One last thought. Some ask me for the Scripture reference that states God wants or expect courage, or success, or growth in ministry. My answer is that those supporting Bible verses may be found right after the ones that tell people to go to church each Sunday, prepare their Sunday school lesson, and commune regularly. The very fact that Scripture reports numbers (and such large ones) ought convince even the simplest that God wants more. His clearest yearnings are maximal: all. Where His work is being done, *He* is at work, and His Word does not return without effect—His intended effect. It was the disciples who were ready to spread a lunch for 14. Jesus fed 5,000. And on Pentecost 3,000 were baptized—not 3.

A word to those who tingle to the words in this book but who have been called to ministries that are unbelievably difficult. Don't give up. Model yourself after the people and stories in this book. Think as they think. First, look to the soil. Perhaps a plow is not the tool for what you are trying to till. Maybe it calls for a jackhammer. If so, get a jackhammer and courageously use it. The 50 have! Which being interpreted is: change your methods. Use what the situation calls for, confident that even in unbelievable difficulties, the Lord's Word will raise up believers and have an effect—His effect.

Second, look to the workman. Decide to improve. The surest and quickest way of improving is seeking out those who do what you think He wants done in your corner of the Kingdom. Seek them and ape their methods shamelessly. There's so much that can be accomplished if we don't think everything must be original. There's no "best" way to make people sit down. Find a way that works for you, and apply it. In doing that you will join an exclusive group— 50 and more who may not really know it but who have developed courageous ministries and *courageous churches* by obeying the Lord's call to faithful service.

Charles S. Mueller, Sr.

Roselle, IL
Courage Day, March 29, 1991

Preface

Grace Church was organized in 1928, just in time for the Great Depression, and for more than 50 years there was concern that this congregation in Bradford, PA, might never move beyond its perilous beginnings.

The town's population slowly shriveled. A major industry shut down. Population shrank further. Later a second plant made major cutbacks, again causing the church and community to lose people.

In the late 60s and 70s, three successive pastors had capably served the small church, but each stayed for only a year or two and then accepted a call to a new location, leaving behind a prolonged vacancy before a new pastor arrived. In spring 1975 Grace was again without a pastor. Average Sunday worship attendance dropped to about 30, and the people voted on whether to close the church's doors forever. Because the decision to remain open passed by only one vote, two weeks later the congregation voted again. Once again by a majority of one they opted to stay open. The church felt uneasy about that decision. Two weeks later they took a third vote. This time 70 percent of the people wanted to stay open and serve the Lord Jesus.

No pastor, old facilities, a declining community—all added up to no future. The situation looked bleak in 1975.

Fifteen years later, Bradford was still on a plateau, or slightly shrinking, but Grace Church was booming. Worship attendance at this vibrant, courageous church exceeded 160 each week. Bible classes abounded. Newly purchased and remodeled facilities enabled Grace to be a community center with ample parking. "The word is out," reported their pastor of nearly 15 years, "if you want to go to a church where things happen, go to Grace. We believe the best years are still to come."

What transformed this dying parish into a living congregation of God's people? What courage explains this dramatic turnaround?

What principles of growth and renewal can be drawn from their experience for you to use, so Grace's story of Christ Jesus building His church may be repeated where you worship? Becoming a courageous church is not a matter of chance, but of choice. What will you choose?

Church members and leaders across the United States and Canada, and even worldwide, do much the same as people in any organization: they compare themselves to their neighbors as one way to evaluate how they're doing—not to measure their faithfulness to God or His mission but rather to measure how effectively they are reaching people. In every denomination, some congregations and pastors do better than others—and the question naturally arises, Why some and not others, especially when all presumably are using the Bible and relying on the same power of the Holy Spirit? This book is not the first to approach the question, but it confirms a hope many share, a hope that not only megachurches of new or nondenominations can grow. Average-sized congregations, the kind many U.S., Canadian, and even British churchgoers attend, also can increase. Nor are the discoveries and dreams we will read about in these stories limited to Lutherans. Every Christian church and leader can put into practice the principles we have distilled from the experiences of these congregations and in some way also be "successful."

A word of explanation is needed: "Successful" here does not automatically mean great numerical growth. In at least one instance it means simply halting the loss of members. "Successful" can also mean making a strong impact on the community. Or it can mean being able to make the transition from serving one ethnic group to serving a different one(s) in the same community. Because of the inherent overtones of the word *successful,* we have chosen to use the word *courageous* (which we'll explain and illustrate later in greater detail). "Successful" tends to focus on results, "courageous" on attitudes—the attitudes necessary to confront the changing sociological scene in America.

Children of the 1950s and 60s don't feel the same loyalty to the past as their parents and previous generations. These baby boomers have lived through technological advances and social changes that made them more particular in their choices, and in how they will spend their time and energies.

16

In *American Mainline Religion: Its Changing Shape and Future* (Rutgers University Press, 1987), sociologists of religion Wade Clark Roof and William McKinney describe the baby boomer generation as searching for self-fulfillment. In terms of religious participation, the boomers seek individual experience. Most do not view beliefs as important unless they can be experienced—and experienced easily.

Roof and McKinney also say baby boomers feel an emancipation of the self, so that duty becomes less important than rights. These individuals think institutions should serve individuals, and not vice-versa. And in a world of growing options, it is obvious that no one can participate in everything—and, therefore, few feel guilty for not participating in any particular organization or event.

Christian marketing analyst George Barna highlights the baby boomer lifestyle in *America, 2000: What the Trends Mean for Christianity,* a report of the Barna Research Group. As people try to pursue all their options, they increasingly seek speed and flexibility. Convenience ranks high for them. With little interest in abstract ideas and nonexperiential events, they seek tangibility and simplicity. They expect quality delivery in performance. In a world saturated with advertising, people naturally are more skeptical about promises and their fulfillment.

Lyle Schaller, the highly respected analyst of the American Protestant church scene, notes that ministry is much more difficult today than 25 years ago. People simply feel less loyalty to churches and denominations. Long-established mainline denominations experience the effects of this phenomenon. Schaller sees declining loyalty to church as part of a general decline in institutional loyalties. The 1950s social pressures have vanished, and churches face a quite different world. Witness, for example, the increase of broken families.

Common wisdom as well as the sociologists of religion clearly understand that the church in North America must deliver effective leadership and ministry; weaknesses and mistakes are not so easily hidden or forgiven as they might once have been. Professional ministry staff people and churches must become increasingly intentional about the ways they offer the Gospel to people. They must be open to new methods of reaching out—and do so other than at the expense of scriptural doctrine.

With that in mind, we, on the basis of a grant from Lutheran Brotherhood insurance group, analyzed the courageous congregations in one denomination (our own, The Lutheran Church—Missouri Synod) to discover and interpret how they carry out effective, exciting ministries in today's new world. These churches either

1. courageously confronted difficult or declining situations; or

2. made courageous decisions and took courageous actions to reach out with the Gospel, and so continued their process of spiritual and numerical growth: of growing up, growing together, growing out, and growing more.

We chose churches for this study from two sources. Most choices derive from a computer-selected list that, in the denomination's annual statistical report, showed increase in recent years

- in annual growth in baptized membership;
- in average worship attendance; and
- in the number of adult accessions.

This method yielded about 200 names.

We omitted denominationally subsidized churches founded after 1980 because we thought their experiences would be less transferable to other churches. (Most newly planted churches, though not all, tend to have fast numerical growth in their first decade.)

We also invited certain regional executives and seminary professors of the denomination to submit names of churches they thought were doing some great ministry in the Lord's name. This garnered an additional 100 congregations. We sent a short questionnaire to the 300 churches and their pastors in this original pool, and received answers from 200. We should also point out that we made no effort to contact those who didn't respond. Though their numerical growth is impressive, they excluded themselves by a lack of response.

Our three-person team studied these questionnaires and looked for powerful stories, memorable statements, and especially, evidence of growth. We recognize that our criteria for stories and statements make our choices subjective. In deciding, at least two of us had to agree on the evaluation. Most often, all three of us independently agreed on the merits of the selection.

We also attempted to represent rural and city, north and south, east and west. Though sometimes several similar churches deserved inclusion, and took the time to complete the form, we could choose only one because of space considerations. From this process, we selected 70 churches for further study. (We thank those churches and their leaders who helped by providing input and regret that all the stories could not be told due to space limitations.)

This smaller group received a second, much lengthier questionnaire, asking the pastor to comment on the following:

- Factors (strengths, weaknesses, opportunities, and threats) involved in growth or redirection
- Changes that precipitated quality growth (internal) and then quantity growth (external)
- How the change process toward growth or redirection began
- "Dark moments" in the journey, with accompanying sources of encouragement
- What each pastor had learned personally from the experience
- How the experience had affected each pastor's personal spiritual life, as well as the congregation's corporate pilgrimage
- What they anticipated for the future

Fifty pastors responded to this second questionnaire. Each was then interviewed by phone for 30–60 minutes. With their permission, the interview was recorded and transcribed so all three of us could read interview results. We also asked them to fill out a final, short questionnaire.

The three questionnaires and the telephone interview with the pastor provided information for these stories, which present their perspective. Our research team tried to use as many stories and references as possible, but we didn't feel compelled to include all 50, nor to give equal length to each. (Here we give special thanks to the Rev. David B. Marth, who conducted the telephone interviews, to Robin Mueller, who helped organize the congregational profiles around the basic principles for growth, and to Kathy Buss, who provided a content analysis of the material on the computer.)

We want this book to encourage and inform others of what God in Christ can and is doing. We heavily emphasized the use of "quotable quotes."

Are these stories representative of a larger number, or are they exceptions? Many lean heavily toward being unusual. We say "unusual" because, sadly, a recent statistical analysis reveals that fewer than 300 of the denomination's 5,990 U.S. congregations (less than 5 percent) shows even a moderate growth of 10 percent or more new members from 1983 to 1985.

Until recently, Lutheranism in America was highly ethnic, not unlike ethnic origins of some other denominations. Germanic and Scandinavian immigrants remained conscious of their nationality and language for several generations. Part of their ethnic identity included the Lutheran faith. As these immigrants settled in various U.S. cities and regions, they founded churches patterned on the ones they had left. Even in the 1950s and 1960s scramble to suburbia, the adult children of these ethnic groups identified themselves as Lutheran and desired to remain Lutheran.

Unfortunately, conventional ministry among loyal Lutherans has not yielded sustained church growth in most parts of the U.S. True, some congregations demonstrated courage during times of special commitment, such as a long-term mortgage on a building project. At the same time, those congregations and their leaders basically followed the conventional, well-worn path traveled by others before them, feeling little need or desire for outreach and caring ministry beyond people like themselves. As a result of this and other factors, total membership in the major Lutheran bodies has declined for several decades.

Some leaders say decline occurs because more people leave through back doors than enter the front—which may point to unmet needs (problems) in Christian care and assimilation. Others say that people do not enter some of Lutheranism's front doors because it does not invite them. Additionally, walking through some of those doors and becoming part of Lutheranism's celebration of God's presence in Word and Sacrament is difficult for reasons not fully recognized or understood. Both may point to unmet responsibilities in evangelism and/or in critical self-analysis.

Many churches we studied struggle with this very serious issue of trying new approaches to worship, church life, and ministry through which the saving Gospel is expressed while holding fast to the centrality of the doctrine of justification by grace through faith in Christ, the doctrine of the means of grace, and the Law/Gospel understanding of the scriptural message. As you read their stories, you can take hope that the struggle to maintain integrity with your heritage while also seeking to find new methods and expressions for ministry is a struggle worth enduring, no matter what your denominational loyalty.

This book intends to help both professional and lay leaders who are restless for change in their church and ministry and who search for insights about principles and processes. We hope you will see yourself in one or several of these courageous stories, dream a new vision for your congregation, and draw some encouragement and confidence for courageous action.

Appendix I lists by state the names, addresses, and phone numbers of the churches who fully participated in this study (though not all are necessarily mentioned in this book). We encourage you to contact those whose stories seem to pinpoint potential guidelines for your congregation's ministry. Talk with them about your own hopes and dreams, ideas and ideals. They will be more than willing to share how God's Spirit has touched their personal lives and those of their people.

As you read through the profiles of courage, here are a few questions to ask of yourself and/or discuss with others:

1. What congregational profile surprised you the most?
2. What story provided a vision of possibilities for your congregation?
3. What questions would you like to ask the profiled congregation to increase your understanding and gain insight in order to create some new directions in your congregation?
4. Whom might you and a group from your church visit to get a close-up look?
5. What cluster of principles from among the six have top priority in your thinking and planning? Does everyone else agree to that priority? How might you achieve consensus?
6. What additional clusters or individual principles would you add from your experience?
7. Broadly, what business are you in? Specifically, what has God in

Christ called your church to be and to do? (See Kent R. Hunter, *Moving the Church into Action* [St. Louis: Concordia, 1989] p. 50.)

8. What are your current church resources (strengths and weaknesses), possible needs to address (opportunities and threats), and possible major goals (satisfactions to offer). (See David S. Luecke, *New Designs for Church Leadership* [St. Louis: Concordia, 1990], p. 136.)

Chapter 1

Defining Courageous Churches: Principles Are Hot, Canned Programs Are Not

Anyone who has seen Me has seen the Father. How can you say, "Show us the father"? Don't you believe that I am in the Father, and that the Father is in Me? The words I say to you are not just My own. Rather, it is the Father, living in Me, who is doing His work. Believe Me when I say that I am in the Father and the Father is in Me; or at least believe on the evidence of the miracles themselves. I tell you the truth, anyone who has faith in Me will do what I have been doing. He will do even greater things than these, because I am going to the Father. And I will do whatever you ask in My name, so that the Son may bring glory to the Father. You may ask Me for anything in My name, and I will do it.

John 14: 9–14

How should courageous churches be defined? First of all, courageous churches are churches; they are people of faith in Jesus Christ; they are people gathered together around God's Word of grace and power and in whom Christ Jesus lives. Yet, as it so often happens, these local gatherings of believers find themselves facing a dark future, a declining and/or aging membership, a changing neighborhood, a turning in of vision, a loss of zeal for the Lord's work, a selfish spirit that results in internal conflict, a departure of youth to other cities and jobs, a whole host of problems or unmet challenges which can turn once vibrant churches into shadows of what once was.

In spite of such challenging circumstance and settings for ministry, the Lord continues to call forth renewal through His Word and by His Spirit. Many churches have responded, have turned corners, have gotten out of spiritual and organizational cul-de-sacs, and have experienced transformation from nongrowth to growth, from maintenance to mission, and from apathy to activity. We define such churches as courageous because, trusting in Christ Jesus, and led by His Spirit, they moved out in new directions; they left behind the way things were, and joyously ventured forth by God's grace and blessing into uncharted waters.

Who are these churches, and how did Jesus accomplish such things in and through them? And what implications do they see for other churches seeking renewal and transformation from the Lord of the church? These are their stories.

The underlying premise in all the stories and profiles is that courageous churches operate from principles, not by chance or by mindlessly following canned programs for growth (though their leaders often select, modify, and shape other people's programs). Leaders of courageous churches tend to function as architects who base and build programs around general principles. They recognize that programs working in one church may not be as effective in another. Instead, they adapt and develop these programs via a refining grid that makes them relevant, useful, and effective for the local church.

An assumption absolutely undergirding this approach is the realization that each congregation is unique. The dynamics surrounding community needs and the special blend of individuals within a church give it a particular dynamic and mission.

Programs aren't the thread of continuity among these courageous churches. Their leaders offer no quick fix or new canned program that activates a passive church or moves maintenance-oriented people into mission. Instead, when evaluating proposed new or adapted programs, the leaders operate with a set of principles which, while not necessarily articulated, they seem to know intuitively.

We studied these courageous churches to cull out the growth principles they follow. While programs in these churches varied significantly from place to place, many amazingly consistent and repeated standards revealed themselves. The church in Maine differs significantly in ministry from the church serving Mexican immigrants in southern Texas. The church in Alaska faces unique challenges compared to the congregation serving people in a small Oklahoma town. The congregation reaching baby boomers in southern California does ministry differently from the one reaching retired people in southern Florida. Yet, as each church serves in its specific setting, several recurring themes emerge. In our research, the following 35 principles seemed to appear over and over. While some overlap exists, we have clustered these principles into six general themes that will serve also as the focus of the next six chapters.

Outward Bound: A Passion for Reaching Out with Christ to People

1. The pastor, staff, and congregational core members are growth-oriented and biased toward outreach with the Gospel to save the lost.
2. Almost all the pastors have an intentional attitude to grow and work specifically for growth in God's kingdom. Outreach is *the* priority.
3. Churches frequently use church growth principles, language, and teachings. Growth permeates their thinking.
4. Most church members foster outreach and growth through relationships in their everyday contacts. They cultivate "web relationships" of friends, relatives, neighbors, co-workers, and fellow students for outreach.
5. The churches tend to emphasize personalized missionary support. This includes short- and long-term mission activity among members.
6. The churches have a heart for reaching the lost, and evangelism takes high priority. Numerous programs for outreach include advertising and frequent use of direct mail.
7. The congregations work at some stage of church planting or creating a satellite ministry.
8. Leaders strongly emphasize providing enough space for min-

istry. They accentuate location, high visibility, and accessibility for their church building.

Spiritual Growth: The Cutting Edge of Change and Courage

9. Church leaders consider Bible study as key to growth. They understand that churches grow because people are growing spiritually through the Word of God.

10. They stress small group ministries that include prayer and spiritual growth.

11. Prayer takes high priority in the pastor's and church leaders' lives and is reflected in the church's corporate lifestyle, which includes prayer lists, prayer services, and prayer chains. Courageous congregations understand the reality of Satan's attacks and the need to prepare for spiritual warfare.

12. Most church leaders teach the concept of spiritual gifts and help members to discover, develop, and use their gifts. Spiritual gifts serve as the criteria for deploying people into *ministry opportunities* rather than just into offices, boards, titles, or committees. These churches often assimilate new members via some type of spiritual gifts' discovery process.

Celebrative Worship: The Drawing Power of Christ

13. These courageous churches usually offer variety in worship services. Worship is celebrative, with at least one service more contemporary or informal. Strong, Bible-centered preaching dominates worship.

14. Worship occurs in a friendly atmosphere. Church members consciously work to become a caring, loving congregation.

15. Worship style and communication methods are receiver-oriented. Members are visitor-sensitive and are open and accepting of guests.

The Christian Leader as Change Agent

16. The lay as well as professional leaders in a courageous church are people of vision. Understanding both broad objectives and specific goals, they present clear direction.

17. The Christian leaders work for change, and the congregations accept change. The leaders understand possible barriers to change and growth, and the churches are flexible in meeting the challenge barriers present.

18. Risk is acceptable and people have permission to fail. In faith in God's promises, the professional and lay leaders try things that seem humanly impossible. The congregations attempt action never taken before.

19. The churches provide staff in anticipation of growth rather than responding to growth that has taken place. Leadership is active, rather than reactive. Often, staff is "home grown" as leaders find people within the congregation and groom them for professional staff positions, into which they are certified.

20. The leaders manage conflict, accepting it as a necessary part of change in a growing congregation. Leaders know how to minister to negative, subjective, nongrowth people who often bare their teeth at meetings. These professional and lay leaders don't allow the "alligators" to set the agenda, though they recognize that some people will disagree with the congregation's direction.

The pastor and other key church leaders possess perseverance.

21. In these congregations, the (senior) pastor considers himself to be, and the church views him as, the congregational leader.

22. The professional leaders equip the laity. They see their primary job as motivating, releasing, and training laity through a preaching and teaching ministry. These leaders strongly emphasize the priesthood of all believers.

23. The professional leaders deal intentionally with people who develop hurt feelings or other negative responses to the growing church. They accept that reaction (and their feelings about it) as part of what happens when serving a church in a courageous manner.

24. The professional leaders strongly attempt to remain on the cutting edge of ministry through continuing education. They constantly look for new ideas, attend seminars, read books, listen to tapes, and often engage in post-graduate work. They also motivate key congregational leaders to do likewise.

A People-Centered Ministry

25. These churches operate to meet their community's felt needs. Each church constantly investigates needs and finds vehicles to touch people's lives in relevant ways.

26. The churches display a positive spirit, usually reflected by the pastor's tone and style. Members feel strong enthusiasm and a sense of renewal. An edifying atmosphere builds people up and encourages them in their faith and Christian life.

27. These churches encourage fellowship and maintain a family atmosphere.

28. The ministry of these churches is relevant, contextual, and indigenous. The community, not the tradition, dictates the ministry style.

29. The churches know about different people groups in the community, and they design ministry and evangelistic strategies accordingly.

30. The churches work diligently to assimilate new people and help them feel at home at various stages along the entry path.

Running the Race: Goals, Plans, and Organization

31. Congregational leaders communicate high expectations for members. People feel strongly committed to the work of ministry in the congregation. Members place the church as a high priority in their lives.

32. The churches operate from a world view that offers choice— in Bible studies, service times, and worship styles.

33. These churches plan. The professional and lay leaders set goals and work toward fulfillment of them.

34. The leaders of these churches organize pragmatically, display a

passion for success and effectiveness, and celebrate goals achieved as victories.

35. The churches sustain growth by change in the organizational relationship between pastor and people, in the structures of congregational decision-making, and in continued self-analysis and redefinition of the ministry philosophy, frequently with the aid of church consultants.

These, then, are the six clusters of principles that organize the following chapters. They will be reviewed again at the end of their respective chapters. We will close our report with reflection on leaders, churches, and culture.

Chapter 2

Outward Bound: A Passion for Reaching Out with Christ to People

This is what is written: The Christ will suffer and rise from the dead on the third day, and repentance and forgiveness of sins will be preached in His name to all nations, beginning at Jerusalem.

Luke 24:46–47

But you will receive power when the Holy Spirit comes on you; and you will be My witnesses in Jerusalem, and in all Judea and Samaria, and to the ends of the earth.

Acts 1:8

Courageous churches are poised for outreach. They possess a growth mentality, which is a major component in their philosophy of ministry. The courageous pastors in our study usually articulate outreach, the lay leaders own it, and many congregational members participate in it.

These churches clearly understand and articulate their purpose. They see direction for their existence rooted in the great commission "to make disciples of all peoples." They receive from Jesus Christ power to go and make disciples, confident of His promise to be with them. They thus demonstrate a growth/action bias. They've captured a vision for looking outward rather than inward. This philosophy and world view permeate the churches' priorities and the activities they pursue.

Of the 50 churches studied in depth, 80 percent have well-organized, intentional visitation programs serving a variety of purposes and people: assimilation, sick and shut-ins, and (for 92 percent of these churches) outreach. Ninety-four percent have evangelism committees (although some pastors questioned if the committee itself is effective).

The greater evangelism strength stems from the fact that 90 of these churches teach evangelism techniques and train people in outreach. Evangelism programs widely used in these churches include "Heart to Heart," "The Master's Plan," "Dialogue Evangelism," and "Evangelism Explosion."

Church-growth thinking significantly influences almost all of these congregations. The term "church growth" generally signifies a church growing up spiritually, growing together in fellowship, growing out numerically, and growing more by planting new missions. Church growth is the opposite of church decline.

Many pastors and churches in this study have been exposed to church growth ways of thinking as well as to the "Church Growth Movement in America." The majority write and speak in a way that reflects conscious commitment and adherence to a disciplined study and application of those factors related to growth in churches at all four levels.

Pastors and other professional leaders frequently refer to church-growth workshops, films, books, and other resources. Some have used church-growth consultants for analysis and guidance. For many pastors, church-growth language makes up part of everyday speech. Many were or had been enrolled in doctor of ministry courses in church growth. One pastor saw his whole ministry change after participating in a two-week church-growth seminar. Another taught the subject for years and then set about applying its principles. Yet another pursued the various parts of the discipline in research and writing projects in earning a doctor of ministry degree in an area other than church growth. And, in most of these 50 churches, lay people as well have learned church-growth principles and practice them.

Changing Attitudes

"I began meeting with the elders right away," reports the Rev. Donald Miles, pastor of St. John, Glendale, NY. "I graphed out the rate of decline over the previous 15 years. Then I drew a straight line projection and showed them that we had about five more years— and then we're gone!

31

"They saw it and agreed to think it could be much different. They proposed that our motto be like Saint Paul's—'all things to all men so that by all possible means I might save some.'"

In this way Miles began to reshape the attitudes of a congregation that was rapidly shrinking in numbers and in influence. God began to set the stage for a turnaround in a church that would come alive in outreach and evangelism.

As this attitude for outreach created by God's Word permeates a congregation, God appears to release the energy of His people toward effective ministries that touch people's lives outside the congregation.

Pastor Christopher Dodge of St. Matthew in Walled Lake, MI, speaks a lot about church growth. His attitude stems from far more than a desire to be successful or to build a large congregation.

Is St. Matthew a courageous church? Dodge answers, "I believe so. It certainly has a lot of courageous people. They're people who are willing to really seek out the Lord's will. They recognize that we're here for a purpose, and that purpose is to reach the lost and disciple them."

Many pastors intentionally move their churches toward developing an attitude of outreach. When the late Rev. Dennis Schiefelbein in Corpus Christi, TX, faced a challenging Hispanic ministry, he knew he had to change attitudes. He sought new, visionary leaders who weren't locked into "traditional modes of thinking."

While leadership seems key to the courageous church, attitudes seem key to leadership.

Our study indicates that attitudes are changed and turned outward by being both taught and caught. Teaching and preaching were the means God used to encourage outreach. Attitudes were also caught because they were modeled. Congregational members reflect the pastor's attitudes. Pastor Jeffrey King of Christ, Southwick, MA, says he used the Word to deliberately reshape attitudes.

"Three years ago, our church was demoralized," says King. "However, I sensed a tremendous potential. The people, stagnant for so long, were ready to try anything! I worked to reshape the attitudes of our congregation through uplifting, contemporary worship celebrations . . . and I found that an enthusiastic attitude was a highly contagious thing!"

St. Mark, in Kentwood, MI, (near Grand Rapids), grew quickly under its first pastor. With its second pastor, it consolidated its gains for nine years. The Rev. Rodney Otto, the third pastor, encountered a church comfortable with itself and lacking interest in growth. Otto worked on an attitude change by encouraging leaders ready for growth and incorporating new mission-oriented leaders. He credits church-growth thinking as bringing about change. A growth-minded pastor spoke at St. Mark's planning workshop. Otto immersed himself in church-growth literature in a doctor of ministry program at a local seminary, implementing part-time staff filled by congregation members. And assistance from various church-growth workshops encouraged self-study.

In order to organize for anticipated and planned-for growth, church leaders not only are changing the organization to streamline decision-making, but also are interested in pursuing two levels of members, with a second category of "friends" or "associate members" for those who are relatively inactive. This represents quite some change in attitude.

Cross of Christ is located in suburban Chattanooga, TN, an area slowly declining, particularly because of major layoffs in one large firm. Yet they've experienced rapid growth—300 percent—in membership in three years. Pastor Edwin Doepel arrived in 1987 after six years experience in the pastoral ministry. His predecessor had been ill for many years, and the church had gradually declined. Attendance dropped from 117 in 1983 to 97 in 1986. The people wanted growth.

A congregation's spirit and direction reflects a pastor's attitude, according to Doepel. "I came with the attitude that I'm going to give it all I've got, and if it didn't work out, I can always move on.

"In my first sermon, I asked one thing from the church—to be given the privilege to make mistakes. If you don't have the privilege of making mistakes, then you're not trying hard enough. When I fall, they don't hold it against me—I think because I was willing to fall pretty vigorously when I went down a few times."

Doepel sees himself primarily as an evangelist. He concentrates first on reaching people related to members, like unchurched spouses—"family members that were just kind of laying around, waiting to be harvested," he says. As new people come in, members grow in excitement. Doepel models excitement, and it becomes contagious.

By the end of his first year, attendance rose to 181. By his second year it was 245, and in the third year it reached 273. Without momentum, a key point in Doepel's view, real growth won't happen. He compares those first years to a jet taking off. "You give it full throttle to lift off the runway, which takes courage. But once you're up, you can cruise."

A critical transition occurs when membership reaches 430 and weekly worship attendance about 240. "The people were getting a little tight-jawed and tight-fisted," Doepel remembers. "I took a bit of a beating at that time. I said to them, 'Do you want me to quit? Do you want us to shut down evangelism, to take the billboards down and take up our street signs?'

"Growth is definitely uncomfortable at first. But you simply put your arms around them and say, 'We're in this together; you're not going to be left behind. We love you and will keep loving you.'

"Outreach ministry is like an addiction. You start reaching some, and you want to reach more. It's just so much fun to see people come to praise Jesus Christ and have their lives renewed, and to develop such a close working relationship with them when they're going through rough times."

Intentionally Growing

Most pastors, usually the lay leaders, and the general church personality demonstrate an intentional attitude toward growth. Rather than *re*acting to the environment within the congregation, these pastors reflect a proactive, shaping style of leadership characterized by strong desire to participate in the growth of God's kingdom.

This dynamic desire that the church take part in the growth of God's kingdom is either implied or strongly stated in these courageous churches. Pastor Ronald Janssen of Holy Cross, Riverdale, GA, doesn't specifically talk about outreach in most sermons. But, he says everything he communicates conveys the impression that outreach ought to be second nature for Christians; if a person is forgiven, that person wants others to experience forgiveness, too. Janssen feels this is caught as well as taught: "It rubs off on other people."

Holy Cross was founded in an Atlanta suburb in 1964. By 1979, the Atlanta area became a resettlement center for Southeast Asian

34

refugees, so three women members intentionally began serving refugees—helping them to get settled, contact doctors, receive food stamps, find jobs, and tackle other challenges people encounter in a new country, even a new area. That intentional social ministry outreach has touched almost 8,000 lives.

Holy Cross' intentional sensitivity to cultures and languages shows in its worship. Normally world evangelization calls for working separately with people groups. But in Holy Cross' case, members did not see that as the course to take in worship. They start with a 15-minute all-Cambodian service of Bible reading, prayers, and sermon followed by the 8:30 Anglo service which incorporates Laotian Gospel reading and sermon. An 11 o'clock Anglo service is also offered. The people themselves want to worship together this way.

The church intentionally reaches out with the offer of new life in Jesus Christ. In one year, Holy Cross celebrated 16 adult converts (most of them Southeast Asians), and the following year and a half 105, 65 of them Southeast Asians and 40 Anglos.

Holy Cross offers Bible study classes in Laotian and Cambodian languages, as well as in English. Average attendance at the multilingual Sunday worship services is 200, up from 150 in 1985. Sunday morning Bible class is at 120, and 270 participate in Bible study during the week. Currently about 40 percent of Holy Cross' members are relatively new Christians.

Besides a part-time case worker and part-time director of resettlement ministry, Holy Cross employs a full-time Laotian lay minister, who is preparing for the pastoral ministry.

The Rev. Ronald Janssen notes that regional and national leaders have greatly encouraged him and Holy Cross' outreach. And, although having sufficient financial resources for these specialized ministries is difficult, the church continues to stretch beyond its limitations. Janssen explains, "The primary question for the people of Holy Cross is whether something is of the will of God or not. If it is, then we ought to do it, and the Lord will provide. That's how I would define a courageous church.

"One example is that the resettlement ministry didn't have enough money for one of the payrolls. Then we got news that Lutheran World Relief is going to give us another grant. This kind of thing happens to us over and over again."

Janssen very much enjoys this ministry, though he had no cross-cultural background. He grew up in an Illinois farm community and was previously at a large church in Fort Wayne. While serving, he was often ill and underwent several kidney transplants. He views his illness as a long, agonizing process of falling short of many expectations.

"What I learned from my ongoing struggles," he believes, "was that I really needed the forgiveness and love of God. I came to this congregation really identifying with the need of people to be forgiven by God. It's important that people can know when they walk into the church with a burdened heart that they can walk out of it with joy.

"I believe Paul was right. He said, 'I have confidence in the Gospel because that is the power of God for salvation.' "

The Rev. Donald Miller of Immanuel Church and University Center in Lawrence, KS, reflects this tone when he says, "I'm strongly committed to the church being vital and alive, active and fulfilling its mission.

"The thing that brings us together is effectively proclaiming Jesus Christ as Savior to our community and sharing Him individually in our lives as well as through the congregation corporately. The Great Commission is the base of this, and everything we do must go back to this base."

Immanuel and the University Center did not always foster outreach as top priority. They were pursuing separate lives in the same town when people began to talk about merger as a course of action so both could survive. Two or more congregations frequently discuss a merger when their membership is stagnant or declining. On paper, creating one larger church makes sense, yet mergers seldom happen. The reason is that the leaders from one or both churches often fear some serious loss—at a minimum the loss of some independence, perhaps their church building, and usually their own unique history and church personality.

Yet some have merged successfully. In 1986, Immanuel and the Student Center at the University of Kansas courageously merged into what became a unified town/gown ministry.

Both the old Immanuel facility and the campus ministry facility needed extensive repair, and it seemed logical to repair just one. The campus facility stands in the middle of town at a heavily used intersection; the Immanuel building was in a less accessible, declining part of town.

Both sacrificed. Immanuel members gave up their building of 55 years and risked domination by a student ministry. The campus ministry sacrificed its independence and student leadership. The resulting unified ministry has gained about 20 percent a year in average church attendance—from a stable combined total of about 180 in the year of the merger, to 203 and 239 in successive years. The original combined membership of 447 has since grown to 590.

No one anticipated such fast growth, and new courage must accommodate accompanying changes. When the congregations merged, Immanuel's pastor of 20 years retired. The present pastor, the Rev. Donald Miller, a 25-year veteran, came about a half year after the merger. After seeing the refurbishing through to completion, he provided the evangelistic thrust that has come to characterize this new ministry.

Newer members find the current growth exciting and want even more; some older members, however, are unsure. Members are moving toward resolving this tension. Miller hopes the church will take the courageous steps necessary to continue growth.

This intentional effort to grow must be felt strongly by the pastor and people because growth often meets resistance. Some people become uncomfortable in a growing church. Strangers appear, and crowded conditions require changes—including those that will affect the members financially.

Pastor Thomas Braun of Family of Christ in Andover, MN, reports that when some leaders began emphasizing community outreach, other members left because they feared the loss of their small family atmosphere. Family of Christ courageously faced the struggle and concluded that the church's mission means reaching out rather than being turned inward.

When confronted with this common reaction, key leaders in a courageous church must intentionally—and overtly—commit their church to growth. Grace congregation was founded in 1932 in Bradford, PA, a small town near the north-central border. Although initially offering a promising future, the population in more recent years dropped due to the closing of a major plant. In the late 60s/early 70s, three successive pastors had capably served the tiny church, but each moved within a year or two, usually leaving a vacancy for a year or more. Many members left, and discouragement was prevalent.

In the spring of 1975, the congregation, with an average attendance of about 30, voted on whether to continue or to close. Since the vote to stay open won by a majority of only one, the congregation voted again two weeks later. Again a majority of one wanted to stay open. After consulting with the district president, the members voted a third time a few weeks later.

This time 70 percent wanted to stay open.

The Rev. J. Arthur Cox arrived that summer fresh from the seminary.

Perhaps because of the combination of the hope that a new pastor brings and officers who felt hope for the future, the attitude of the majority of the people changed significantly. The remaining old-timers especially wanted to cooperate and to do whatever was necessary for ministry. They gave their total support to the pastor and new council.

Grace experienced slow but steady growth, despite a shrinking community. In 1983 attendance averaged 118, and by 1988 it rose to 157, with momentum increasing in the past several years. Adult confirmations rose from four a year to 21 in 1988.

Pastor Cox attributes most of the change to building the church around adult Bible study. The original Sunday morning class of six members quickly grew to 20. Now the church holds four weekly Bible classes and three cell groups; average weekly attendance is 96. Cox says the church's backbone was and continues to be Bible study.

Two additional major changes helped Grace's numerical growth. In the early 1980s, the church purchased and remodeled a vacant, 15,000-square-foot A&P grocery store in the middle of town—certainly a courageous act for a small church with no money for such an investment.

The members spent a year-and-a-half gutting the building. When the money promised for remodeling didn't materialize and they faced bankruptcy, they raised $55,000 among churches in the district, which resulted in an impressive building.

It was after moving into the new building that another major local employer cut its work force and the church lost 40 members—including half the young couples who had worked so diligently for the new building. Grace Church had ample reason to give up the dream during those years. Indeed, at one point Cox wondered if he would leave next. "We were sustained, however, by the knowledge that we were doing the Lord's work and that somehow He would provide. No one lost hope. We all knew that it would not be easy, but we were convinced that we were doing what the Lord wanted us to do and therefore He would make it all happen," Cox confessed.

A second major change for Grace was when the church and its leaders participated in a two-year church-growth process under the direction of a church-growth consultant. Grace began to see all sorts of new possibilities for ministry and to learn the how-to for doing it. Although Bradford was small and declining, 40 percent of its people were unchurched. The field was ready for harvest. The people of Grace had a great attitude for outreach with the Gospel and a desire for being the friendliest church in town. Now they got the tools for growth.

Part of Grace's self-study included a visit to St. Paul's in Trenton, MI, to study their spiritual gifts administration program. With this as a point of reference, Grace added a director of spiritual gifts, a woman member who greatly desired to serve. Now, 50 percent of Grace's members participate in at least one aspect of the congregation's ministry.

Cox explains that, as the people changed, he had to change. This meant a greater willingness to delegate more work and to increase his administrative responsibilities. But he knows that's necessary for Grace's continued growth.

In retrospect, Cox wishes he had begun earlier to involve lay people in hands-on ministry. His waiting left many needs unmet.

Grace definitely intends to continue to grow. In 1988 Grace Church purchased two adjacent small houses for expanded parking; in 1990 Grace purchased two more buildings. Now it looks forward to buying two other properties. Grace also plans to add staff in education and music.

Grace Church enjoys an increasingly positive reputation. Cox says the word is out: If you want to go to a church where things happen, go to Grace. He speaks with evident excitement and expectation, insisting that the members deserve the credit, that they've come a long way from the days when 30 people seriously considered closing the church. Now they believe the best years are still to come. "They're absolutely convinced that their purpose in life is to reach out with the Gospel."

St. Peter in Brooklyn, NY, intentionally attempts to adapt to other cultures. St. Peter's history began in 1897, but its neighborhood of Cypress Hills changed ethnically and racially in the 1970s as children of white homeowners moved to Long Island and new homeowners tended to be Hispanic and black. In one decade the population of 40,000 changed from 97 percent white to 80 percent nonwhite. And the congregation, at one time 99 percent Anglo, has changed to just 20 percent Anglo, and serves people from 12–15 different lands.

St. Peter's leaders view change as opportunity and make strong financial and leadership commitments to outreach. They want the church to adapt as the community changes. And when the congregation called the Rev. David Benke in 1975 to be its pastor, the leaders included a plea to develop the church into a viable congregation of the 21st century. They "granted permission" to Benke to try innovative ministry in order to reach the community.

Changes include continuous openness to people of different cultures and worship styles, and diverse forms of worship. Benke explains, "Where the climate was kind of Germanic, old time, we just took out the stuffiness a little bit and warmed it up. We allow, especially in Spanish, open prayer and open time for statements of faith, and a long, long handshake of peace, a long and chaotic free time."

The English service varies, and every other week follows the conventional, liturgical worship of the Lutheran hymnal, including the chants. The Spanish service, however, is always informal. If somebody wants to pray, the service stops and that person prays for another. Benke describes it as a "rock and roll service. It's a lot of fun."

(It should be added that Hispanics are not the only culture served. A growing proportion of the neighborhood is Indian, with Hindu or Muslim background—and many participate in St. Peter's Bible studies in home groups and cottage meetings.)

"We've learned that attention to the basics in terms of relationship development inside the Word-Sacrament community is what pays off," says Benke. "We've learned to trust our teachings, even as we're surrounded with all kinds of different ideas.

"We've learned that people who come from different cultures cannot only get along but can thrive in a united Body of Christ as long as we pay attention to differences without being paralyzed by them."

Courageous churches develop a lifestyle centered around outreach and growth. Growth does not originate solely from an annual event, a particular program, or a specific committee or board's concern. Key leaders constantly communicate intentional growth. The members' Christ-centered lifestyle, which includes much faith-talk, promotes growth.

Seeing with "Church-Growth Eyes"

Arvada, CO, a well-established suburb of Denver, has almost reached its growth potential. King of Kings, begun in 1973, had 684 baptized members by 1981. Attendance, though, averaged just 110.

A change began in 1983 during a yearlong vacancy, when church leaders realized that change was necessary if the church was to witness effectively to the community.

Today membership stands at 725, while attendance has risen to 250. Growth currently averages about three families per month. A 25 percent increase in attendance happened in 1988 by adding a second service.

The Rev. Tom Teske, a 1970 seminary graduate, came as pastor in 1984, ending King of Kings' one-year vacancy. In his judgment the most significant factor sparking the change and growth at King of Kings was his involvement in the doctor of ministry program at Fuller Theological Seminary, especially in courses on growth, evangelism, renewal in the church, and small group ministry.

"The focus I caught from professors and fellow students of many different backgrounds was contagious enough that the congregational leaders very quickly began to see the church's ministry 'through church growth eyes.'"

Two leaders also attended a church-growth workshop and came back strongly committed to revitalizing the congregation's mission. Congregational members also attended Great Commission convocations, which gave them more outreach motivation and helped the congregation develop its mission statement, "Making Disciples Who Love and Serve," which affects most activities.

41

Teske places heavy stress on Bible study, insisting that the congregation couldn't grow numerically until it began with inner growth in Scripture. He strongly encourages Sunday morning class involvement as well as various evening studies. The church holds 10 adult Bible study classes.

If he were beginning again, Teske would involve more leaders in parachurch training workshops in growth, outreach, and evangelism. He feels their enthusiasm ignited the spark in the rest of the congregation.

Involving lay people requires substantial administration. Teske says, "It's by and large putting ideas in people's minds and letting them take and go with it. It's kind of fun when it works, but frustrating when it doesn't."

Perhaps the most meaningful outcome of church growth thinking is the overall perspective gained. Pastor Teske talks about receiving "new eyes." Soon everything in ministry and church life relates to the goal of growth fueled by the attitude of outreach. As Teske observes, this new focus on God growing His church becomes contagious through others' excitement in experiencing God-given growth. Soon pastor and people begin thinking, "Why can't we do that?"

Lamb of God, Humble, TX, is located in a suburb of Houston which once had experienced rapid growth, growth that now has slowed.

Founded in 1977 by the Rev. John H. Miller (a 1965 seminary graduate with a doctor of theology degree in the Old Testament), the congregation grew annually by 5–10 percent. Worship attendance grew from 329 to 451 during a 5-year period. In 1989, 80 of its members launched a new mission church in a nearby suburb (Kingwood).

Miller strongly believes that the primary factor in Lamb of God's growth stems from his introduction to how-to-grow-a-church through a two-week course under C. Peter Wagner in 1979. He feels that the course combined with all the reading he did changed his path of ministry and the course of Lamb of God.

"I got 'church growth eyes,'" he says. "I began to see our problems in overall outreach and assimilation. I began to help our people understand that everything we do has to do with reaching out with

Christ to people. I came to realize that outreach is not a program—it's a way of doing ministry."

Outreach means gaining a vision from God's Word of what God can do in His churches. Participants learn this from reading, hearing, and seeing actual growth that occurs in countless Christian churches of all denominations. "My church-growth training gave me a great deal of confidence about what needed to be done and how to do it. We constantly held up to people our purpose—fulfilling the Great Commission—and the power of God's promises, so that nothing could sidetrack us from our goal."

The economic bust of the mid-1980s tested the leaders' commitment to continued growth. The oil boom of earlier years had showered them with benefits. But then many members moved away, general income dropped, the congregation had trouble meeting its commitments.

The congregation seriously considered (briefly) deferring its plans to build a new sanctuary, but they forged ahead anyway. They also added another pastor to the staff to help facilitate growth. And Lamb of God grew in numbers in spite of the economy.

Half of Lamb of God's members are solidly involved in ongoing congregational ministries. The congregation recently added an administrative assistant, who spends hours on the phone recruiting people for various programs and then tracking their involvement, especially if they're new.

Miller doesn't feel he's overly creative, but that he's very good at adapting programs to fit his particular congregation and setting. He says a great strength in the kingdom of God is that pastors share what they've discovered. He owes a great deal to other pastors of growing churches, and he eagerly shares his materials with others, particularly in his consultant role to other churches.

What about discouraging times? "Our encouragement came mainly from knowing we were doing what Christ had sent us to do [make disciples] and that, since this was ultimately His work, He was in charge," says Miller. "Whatever the result, then it was up to Him.

"We gave our best, as faithful stewards of God's gifts should. We worked very hard. We celebrated where we could celebrate and didn't dwell on setbacks. I'm convinced that His Spirit is at work among us, as I saw again with the establishment of the Kingwood mission. Christ has taken care of His work as we have done our job without undue attention to all the negative things that could have happened."

Cultivating a Church to Serve

The Rev. Elmer Thyr considers himself a church planter. He began new churches three times since beginning his pastorate in 1952. He's now cultivating the growth of Shepherd of the Hills in Rancho Cucamonga, CA, which he founded in 1978 in this rapidly growing community in eastern Los Angeles. In 1989 attendance at Shepherd of the Hills averaged about 360. Thyr says growth has been steady but not spectacular because the community has high turnover.

A congregation's first building, says Thyr, should be called "our chapel" and not "our church" so that the new people join current members in the dream that this congregation will be serving *thousands*. Once a church clarifies its position, every other action becomes more and more obvious.

Thyr thinks Paul's statement, "I have become all things to all men so that by all possible means I might save some," certainly applies to Shepherd of the Hill's mission. The church's goal emphasizes reaching the unchurched and unsaved.

To carry out that mission, Shepherd of the Hills relates to people where they are, spiritually as well as physically. Thyr uses publicity and advertising as part of his strategy to attract people to the church the first time. His interest in printed outreach began in his first mission 39 years ago. A member there, a high school print shop teacher, looked for projects his kids could accomplish, and the church benefited from their efforts.

Thyr considers mailings especially important at Christmas and Easter to make the church constantly visible to the community. "Don't expect too much the first time," he cautions. "Repetition makes the difference—at least seven times. Constantly bombard people with brochures and other mailings."

In a recent pastor's class, 10 new members said they learned about the church through Christmas, Easter, or some other mailings.

Sometimes reaching out to people with Christ means reaching to unchurched children through a school and to member families who begin to fall away from Christ.

The Rev. Dennis Kastens of Good Shepherd in Collinsville, IL, considers himself well-versed in church-growth approaches. He thinks Good Shepherd can be a trendsetter for others in two ways.

"Develop a school as a tool for church growth," he says. (But, based on previous as well as current experience, he feels an adequate tuition is crucial so that the school won't divert money from other growth programs.) Good Shepherd especially makes new contacts through their preschool and through their day care. Their total school goal is to enroll 800 students.

The other trendsetting approach Good Shepherd encourages is prevention of back-door losses by following up with members who have been absent from worship for several weeks. The pastors prepare the list from visual and personal contact on Sunday morning. By 1 p.m. Sunday, a lead elder calls in for names and then distributes them to other elders for follow-up. An elder telephones them as soon as they'll answer the phone, but definitely no later than Tuesday. Those who are absent four consecutive weeks, Kastens visits, usually on Sunday afternoon. He doesn't confront their absence, but shares information about what's happening at the church. Because the approach extends a Gospel-oriented effort to care, Kastens and the elders feel that people appreciate these contacts.

Cultivating growth consciousness to permeate every aspect of congregational life can be done, but not overnight. Dr. Paul W. Meyer developed and directed a program for directors of Christian education at Christ College, Irvine, CA, for a number of years, where he taught church growth and evangelism. Originally a day-school teacher himself, he was ordained into the pastoral ministry in 1978.

While full-time on the Christ College faculty, Meyer served Salem in Orange part-time as an assistant pastor for seven years. In the past two years he switched roles to become full-time senior pastor at the church and part-time teacher at Christ College.

Salem, founded in 1972 as a mission offshoot of the very large St. John's in Orange, once had 400 members. By spring 1982 Salem had less than 60 active members, and church leaders felt they might have to close during the summer. They decided instead that they needed an assistant pastor who could help preach, teach, evangelize, and plan. That's when Meyer became the assistant pastor. Now Salem has 520 members and a regular worship attendance of 235. Its school, started in 1983, enrolls 395 students.

The school and church are financially separate, though the

church makes a major contribution to the school, and 44 of the 163 school families attend the congregation's worship services. A close working relationship exists between school and church staffs. All teachers are congregational members and meet weekly with Meyer. They work particularly close together when any family shows an interest in the Lord.

Meyer describes himself as a serious student of the factors related to growth of churches. After teaching the principles at Christ College for 10 years and conducting more than 100 weekend seminars on growth, he now personally applies what he taught. He explains that God said it was time to get off the podium and put these principles to work.

Salem's small congregation had three kinds of people, according to Meyer. The founders had Midwestern roots, high respect for the pastor, and contentment with a low-expectation, low-energy church. The second group, young professionals and engineers, had high expectations and were willing to pay for improvement. Highly visible Orange County leaders, who were embarrassed by Salem and wanted it to succeed, made up the third group.

How did the growth momentum get restarted? According to Meyer, personal conviction, prayer life, hard work, risk-taking, and determination ranked high from the outset. The goal of growth meant concentrating on worship style, offering sermon encouragement, and turning council and boards into real planning and implementation bodies.

A lay leader told Meyer they used to wonder how he would work church growth into a council-meeting meditation. They expect it now.

They also celebrate whenever possible—new members, Baptism, an especially good offering or attendance, a new Sunday school teacher.

"If I were to state my job description," says Meyer, "it would be to ask the Lord for the vision, then refine it through the committees, and finally get the congregation to adapt and adopt it. And the vision is never static."

He notes that there are some lonely prayer nights when he asks himself, "Am I willing to risk this vision, and willing to pay the cost to enact it?"

Through their planning process, growth goals remain clear.

Salem wants to grow each year by 90 members (or 30–33 families). Next year they intend to add a half-time associate, a year later a third worship service, and the following year will concentrate on re-modeling the church to seat 350.

"We take risks! Risks in praying for a vision. Risks in leadership presenting the vision and letting the leadership adapt and finally adopt a vision. Risks in managing the committees so that, so far as it is possible, no committee fails. Risks in innovation.

"It takes courage, the courage of faith. Dare I pray for this growth? Dare I trust God for this growth? Dare I trust my professional learning and instincts for this growth?"

How does Meyer's full-time life as a pastor differ from his full-time life as a professor? "A surprise, even to me, is that I read a lot more," he answers. "I read a lot both in preparation for worship, and in just keeping a pulse on the future, where I perceive our new prospects are coming from."

Experienced in camping, the Rev. Ronald Goodsman thought Grace in De Witt, IA, should organize its own summer camp in order to strengthen its service and outreach to youth. (Grace originally had mostly older members.) After his installation in May 1983, he established the camp that summer, which has grown ever since. While 350 people of all ages attend the summer camp, 300 teenagers attend the winter camp—a significant number, considering that De Witt high school enrolls only 360.

This ministry, however, did not slow Grace's continuing service, notably to older people and to church workers experiencing difficulties in their lives. Therefore, Goodsman suggested that the church offer a home for the elderly next to the church and/or a guest house for church workers with troubles.

In summer 1988, in a year of drought including farm upheavals and bankruptcies, the congregation displayed their courage to serve by buying property for both. In three special voter's meetings, they first bought a house across the street; two weeks later, they bought two more houses in order to begin a retirement home. And, just two weeks after that, they bought a farm to use for their outdoor ministry. (They had wanted to buy camp property several years earlier, but Goodsman advised waiting until congregational unity was better established.)

Reflecting on Grace's church growth, high mission giving, and commitment to outreach and service projects, Goodsman says, "My goodness, if we can do these things in De Witt, imagine the things they could do someplace else."

Witnessing through the "Web" Concept

Courageous churches often teach the principle of the "web" concept. A congregation establishes a web movement when large numbers of members pray for unchurched people they know through personal contacts. Church members pray for the cultivation of these relationships so that they might have opportunity to share their faith with these everyday contacts. In many congregations, the members are trained to do so through a "Lifestyle Evangelism" training program.

As individuals learn the web principle and witness its powerful impact on outreach for God's kingdom, the local congregation becomes more visitor-sensitive in its worship. Most of these courageous churches demonstrate that lifestyle.

The Rev. Richard Elseroad of Good Shepherd in Gardendale, AL, says the web principle prevails there. People who make growth in God's kingdom a personal priority do invite their friends, relatives, neighbors, co-workers, and fellow students to worship. "That's the key to our growth," explains Elseroad. "Our growth hasn't been explosive; it's just steady. We go over and over this. I encourage people through the bulletin. I ask them to suggest a name. I'll also ask them to bring someone to the next class. Once they've brought someone to class, I'll ask those people to think about bringing someone. I'll ask them to pray for someone. I just keep emphasizing this."

Good Shepherd did not always use the "Web Principle." The congregation began as a mission in 1980. Elseroad, the first pastor, arriving fresh from the seminary to serve this core group of strongly traditional Lutherans, was initially reluctant to introduce changes or innovations.

Growth was slow, with few transfers in. Then Elseroad broadened his philosophical outlook from serving merely the existing Lutherans to reaching all people for and in Christ, including lapsed Christians from other denominations. "The important thing we emphasize and reemphasize is that a person has a relationship with Jesus Christ," explains Elseroad. "As a Gospel-oriented church, we contrast with some of our more legalistic local churches. As soon as we were able to break free from the notion that we were to make these people like us ('and if they didn't like it they could go elsewhere'), we began growing."

Elseroad views receiving the first new adult member from a non-Lutheran background as the springboard that launched Good Shepherd's growth. Then new members began witnessing to friends and relatives. The 'Web Principle' guided our growth. In 1983, attendance averaged 90; by 1989, it had grown to 187—with 20- and 30-year-olds dominating church membership.

What did he learn through this ministry experience and what would he do differently? "I wouldn't have been so tradition-bound," says Elseroad. "I would make changes more quickly than I did before, and not agonize so much over everyone's opinions. I would ask myself what God wants me to do, and less often, what the church . . . [or denomination] . . . wants me to do. I would have gotten to know my community better right from the start.

"As a Lutheran church with its Gospel-oriented message and beliefs and with the forgiveness of sins, we are poised to reach a lot of people who have some kind of Christian religious background but who have never really understood the Gospel because it was mingled with the Law. If we can do a little bit of adjustment to our worship services to make it even more relevant to their situation, I think we're in a good position."

Leaders like Elseroad emphasize and express outreach and growth so often that people under the Spirit's influence internalize its importance. The Lord changes an individual's lifestyle, which in turn transforms the congregation's lifestyle.

Personalizing Missions

A passion to reach out to people with Christ spawns an interest in missions, which takes various forms. Many of the courageous congregations correspond with—and financially support—individual missionaries, and these missionaries often visit and report to them. Individuals within congregations regularly pray for these missionaries. Church bulletin boards carry pictures of missionaries and their families. Newsletters reflect correspondence from them.

Personalized mission support also shows itself in the growing number of mission festivals these churches sponsor, which seems to bring about an overall increase in giving to missions because the members are encouraged by their personal ownership in mission.

Several congregations have taken short-term mission trips to provide support on the field. For example, The Rev. Warren Arndt of Faith in Troy, MI, reports that over 40 members of Faith have been involved in mission outreach in such countries as Brazil, Kenya, China, the Philippines, and South Africa. This outreach has included building projects, street witnessing, VBS projects, and evangelism training for the local church leaders.

For years Arndt has taken advantage of conferences and seminars across the country on church growth. He's also visited many growing churches, always evaluating how principles and programs might fit Faith.

At times he's discouraged by wanting things to move more quickly than they usually do. Reflecting on courage, Arndt says, "I think a courageous church is one that understands its own authority and the culture in which the church resides and is willing to create programs, ministries, styles, and functions that relate innovatively and relevantly to that culture. And, while doing so, it still stays sound to the doctrine and heritage of the church body it represents.

"I think on the whole Faith congregation has been open to the wind of the Spirit as it has flowed through our midst to address the needs of our community and the hurts and pains of our membership as well as the people we are trying to reach. They've been willing to step outside the norm, if need be, in a style of ministry which demonstrates the ability to touch people.

"More and more of our members are becoming bolder in faith and willing to risk facing change to be God's church in action. I hardly ever hear, 'We can't do that.' When they see their own spiritual pilgrimage and hear the testimony of others, it spurs them on to believe that God can and will do some great things through their witness and life."

Living Evangelism

The churches we studied reflect a strong heart for reaching the lost—at home as well as overseas. They offer various programs for outreach because no one particular program can encompass everything that needs to be done in evangelism. Rather, evangelistic outreach permeates all ministry.

Many of these churches' evangelism programs emphasize "Life-style Evangelism" activities that capitalize on relationships through the web concept already noted.

The Rev. Stephen Wagner, pastor of Prince of Peace, Carrollton, TX, authored a widely used relational evangelism program called *Heart to Heart*. "We got to this point through establishing an evangelism style that is appropriate for our kind of people at Prince of Peace," recounts Wagner. "That means a strong emphasis on lifestyle evangelism and relational evangelism. Out of this, *Heart to Heart* evolved."

Many people in Prince of Peace practice this approach to evangelism. "We found we could involve a large number of people from within the congregation and really call them to the evangelistic task. They had the resources to meet those needs and draw people toward themselves on the basis of their interests. It was very well received here, and that's how *Heart to Heart* began."

"Life-style Evangelism" encourages planned, nonconfrontational interaction with unchurched people that builds trust among the unchurched and involves many church members in courageous witnessing.

Even though Wagner wrote the book and most members learn its content, he varies the application of *Heart to Heart* to meet the needs of the congregational group studying it, especially for the Sunday school, which uses a follow-up system to assure an ongoing visitation list.

Some churches use outreach that does not require a specific resource training kit. The Rev. Terry Tieman of Bethel in Fort Smith, AR, says that the 16 people in Bethel's evangelism group are called "kingdom workers." These workers go out in pairs on Sunday afternoons and Monday evenings, making friendly calls on visitors within 48 hours of their first attendance at worship.

Because the northern edge of Detroit reached Immanuel, Mount Clemens, MI, the church works hard at making itself known in the community. They send a number of high-quality mailers to local residents each year, and they draw special attention with an electric message board in front of the church. Pastor Michael Lutz sums up, "I firmly believe that with our location, our congregation can become a very large influence within the community. In order for this to happen we're going to need to trustfully take many steps of faith not knowing exactly what the future will bring."

Planting and Multiplying

While not many churches interviewed were planting churches now, many plan to. Almost half the pastors interviewed indicated some desire to extend the Kingdom by starting another church.

The Rev. Alan Bachert at King of Kings in Chesterfield, MO, while leading his congregation through a building project, wants to plant a satellite congregation in a nearby location, where under the supervision of staff and boards King of Kings can more effectively reach people. Bachert's vision of a multipoint campus and growth attitude enables him to see that mission opportunities exist beyond a building program. His concern for reaching the lost is underscored by the addition of a full-time minister of discipleship to continue the equipping of the saints for this purpose.

Many churches involved in church planting do not identify it as such. They simply start an additional worship service, using an alternative style that targets a type of people in their community different from those the congregation currently reaches. This becomes the easiest, most inexpensive way to start new churches. Churches are planted within churches by providing worship at an alternative time with an alternative style.

This, too, reflects the attitude and philosophy toward growth and outreach permeating these churches as they seek God's will through new ministry.

Building for People

Churches that emphasize people over buildings understand that their buildings are a means to the end of making disciples. They reflect this courageous value in many ways.

First, they know the role space plays in ministry. When space in the sanctuary or the parking lot is cramped, people make sacrifices to enlarge it. Motivated by an outreach attitude, they not only create enough parking space for expansion, they also designate certain spots for "Visitors."

Second, these churches also pay attention to access. They post directional signs within their facility and, demonstrating that they want visitors to experience accessible worship, they often print out their entire worship service.

Third, visibility plays a major role in their outreach. Pastor Michael Lutz of Immanuel in Mount Clemens, MI, says Immanuel placed an electronic sign on its busy road both to advertise church activities as well as to symbolize that Immanuel is there not for itself but the community. Like other indicators of a growth attitude, the sign demonstrates the "outward bound" nature of Immanuel.

Perspective

This pervasive "outward bound" attitude describes these churches. This makes them courageous. This powerfully fuels vital, growing ministries. Dr. Paul W. Meyer of Salem, Orange, CA, reflects the impact that outreach thinking makes on ministry. Having a goal of growth means concentrating on meeting needs, offering encouragement in sermons, and persuading councils and boards to function more effectively based on growth goals.

Meyer advocates and exemplifies a pastor's strong leadership, though the process is far from solitary. The pastor who intentionally reaches out struggles with what God intends for the congregation, refines the vision by interacting with many members, and oversees the effort until it integrates into all of church life.

That a pastor would set out purposefully to achieve growth seems offensive to some ministers in nearly every church body where outreach efforts occur. Meyer, well experienced in outreach and growth issues, presents the other side. He points out that assertive, outreach pastors are out ahead of the people, raising sights, and asking them to try new action. Consequently, failure is more overt than in ministries where goals aren't so challenging. Jesus frequently blesses these efforts. The study of growth in other churches can help build confidence to make the attempt.

Here again are the outward bound principles profiled in chapter 1 that have helped many churches facing an uncertain future to turn the corner:

● The pastor, staff, and congregational core members are growth-oriented and biased toward outreach with the Gospel to save the lost.

- Almost all the pastors have an intentional attitude toward growth and work specifically for growth in God's kingdom. Outreach is *the* priority.
- Churches frequently use church growth principles, language, and teachings. Growth permeates their thinking.
- Most church members foster outreach and growth through relationships in their everyday contacts. They cultivate "web relationships" of friends, relatives, neighbors, co-workers, and fellow students for outreach.
- The churches tend to emphasize personalized missionary support. This includes short- and long-term mission activity among members.
- The churches have a heart for reaching the lost, and evangelism takes high priority. Numerous programs for outreach include advertising and frequent use of direct mail.
- The congregations work at some stage of church planting or creating a satellite ministry.
- Leaders strongly emphasize providing enough space for ministry. They accentuate location, high visibility, and accessibility for their church building.

Chapter 3

Spiritual Growth: The Cutting Edge of Change and Courage

> If you hold to My teaching, you are really My disciples. Then you will know the truth, and the truth will set you free.
>
> John 8:31–32

How or why do churches—even courageous churches—grow? That's an underlying question in many church-growth discussions. We must never forget the central theological truth about church growth: that the *Holy Spirit* "calls, gathers, enlightens, and sanctifies the whole Christian church on earth" (to use Martin Luther's terms).

When people come to faith and grow spiritually in relationship to Jesus, grow together in fellowship, grow out numerically, and grow more by planting new missions, the Holy Spirit is the mover. The apostle Paul, the greatest church leader of all time, kept this belief clear in his thinking and writing. In talking about the Corinthian church, he recognized, "I planted the seed, Apollos watered it, but God made it grow" (1 Cor. 3:6).

The only sure way to prepare for the Holy Spirit's movement is to depend on God's Word and Sacraments, God's means of grace, the means by which the divine enters into our human efforts, directs, and energizes them. The Word of God is our seed to plant.

Nearly all the courageous churches in our study draw people closer to the Scriptures for spiritual growth. Most of these churches report an increasing number of people in Bible study, a greater priority for prayer, and consequently a greater desire to do God's will of mission and ministry by the Holy Spirit's leading, especially through the discovery, development, and use of their gifts of grace.

When interviewed, almost all the pastors echoed the importance and priority of getting people into God's Word. These courageous congregations provide many opportunities and styles of Bible study for members. Among these courageous churches, 36.5 percent of the membership participate in regular Bible study in an average of 13.65 weekly Bible study groups in homes almost as often as at church.

The groups use various materials, frequently mentioning LifeLight from Concordia Publishing House, Crossways, Bethel Bible series, the Navigators 2:7 series, and Serendipity materials.

These courageous churches also accentuate prayer as a major spiritual component. In 72 percent of these churches, members formally organize congregational prayer opportunities beyond public worship. They set up prayer chains, cell groups, prayer partner ministries, prayer ministry teams, prayer workshops, and prayer support groups for the staff.

The third dimension of spiritual growth at the cutting edge centers in spiritual gifts. An astounding 80 percent of these churches teach about spiritual gifts. Most churches use a special questionnaire to identify members' gifts in order to involve the members in church life. Of these 50 churches, 76 percent go so far as to engage someone for the specific task of matching individuals' gifts and talents with ministries either organized by the church or initiated by the individual.

How or why do courageous churches change from nongrowth to growth, from maintenance to mission, from apathy to activity? Bible study, prayer as priority, and the use of spiritual gifts—these are at the cutting edge of change and courage and generate vibrant, relevant and growing ministries. These components form the focus for many stories of courage which comprise the rest of this chapter.

Growing in God's Word

"If you're not growing in the Word, you're dying on the vine," says Pastor John Miller of Lamb of God, Humble, TX. This attitude typifies the pastors, leaders, and corporate lifestyle of these courageous churches. A priority for Bible study encourages members to regularly study the Word and to apply it in their everyday lives.

Many pastors model this. "The pastoral devotional life is something important to me," says Miller. "I've been especially impressed by the importance of prayer in building myself in my own ministry."

The priority for Bible study enhances the pastors' lives and ig-nites lay people's enthusiasm. Martin Hauser, the past congrega-tional president of Tallmadge Lutheran, Tallmadge, OH, explains, "We've touched on the basic, old-fashioned Lutheran belief that expresses a commitment to Bible study and growth through learning and education in the Word.

"In this church we're getting into the Word and studying it rather than being just preached to. That means that our pastor's role has changed dramatically over the years. He's no longer just a preacher, he's now a preacher-teacher.

"The thing that pleases me most, coming from an old time Lu-theran background, is that we average somewhere in the neigh-borhood of 80 members on Sunday mornings in Bible class. These aren't people who are dropping their kids off for Sunday school and going on to breakfast."

This layman also notes significant change in the Word's rele-vancy to lives. "We're not just talking about making sure everybody understands the story or the biblical facts; we're making clear that the Bible is very real and is something that relates to today."

Faith congregation in Troy, MI, also places a high priority on Bible study. Pastor Warren Arndt's special joys include preaching and teaching the Bible in the worship service. "What I try to do is to have their eyes work as well as their ears and hands," Arndt said. The sermon is in printed outline form in the bulletin, with at least five to eight blank spaces with the answer words down in a little bottom section. At least 75 percent of the members bring their Bibles to worship so they can be directed to open the Word and use it. In a majority of sermons, Arndt invites people to respond; sometimes they bow their heads in prayer, sometimes members might be asked for a show of hands in answer to a question. From the Bible, from the fill-in outline, Faith has gone through many books of the Bible.

Arndt briefly describes his method: "We will spend time, usually in the message, trying to pinpoint the specific problem, the sin, and whatever it is that the Lord's talking about in that Scripture. We will also address where the remedy is found. How was it laid out? What does the application mean for us today? I usually call for some kind of action."

Not every church will be open to sermonic Bible studies. Faith, however, was open to this style of preaching and has been spiritually blessed by it.

At Salem in Orange, CA, Pastor Paul Meyer tried a new form of preaching "one summer and it didn't work—either my style (of delivery) or the people's style (of listening didn't blend). We call it an experiment. Then I tried it with Genesis and it worked. I tried Luke, and now I think I'll be an exegetical preacher. I'm beginning to collect books on Exodus so I can do it in the future. The people really seem to respond, too. What's interesting is we're getting a number of old Lutherans to transfer back; that is, folks who were Lutherans, but looked for more biblical preaching for the last 15 years. Now the word has spread. We had an unexpected blessing in September when four couples who were once Lutherans came to our exegetical preaching service, and now they are back in the fold. They express enormous gratitude for this style."

Whether it's exegetical/sermonic preaching, expository preaching, or whether it's Bible classes in home or church, on weekday mornings or evenings or on weekends, they all emphasize spiritual renewal through the Word. St. John's in Glendale, a community in the Borough of Queens, New York City, was founded by German immigrants in 1844. Glendale, once a white community, has become multiracial and multicultural in recent years. For years, no new housing has been built there.

Rev. Donald Miles serves St. John's. When he arrived, he had just graduated from the seminary, after previously holding a major management-level position. At age 46, he knew how to lead.

Miles found the congregation with no children (despite having a parochial school), no teenagers, and only four or five people under age 45. Instead, he saw only about 85 gray-haired, ethnically German people each Sunday morning.

Miles assessed the situation. Belief among the few "younger" members seemed nominal. Visitors never returned. Baptized members had dropped from 1,147 in 1960 to 376 in 1980. Even the most optimistic could see the church would soon die unless something drastic happened.

Self-doubt and humility had replaced the pride in self which other pastors had noted during the 1970s. According to Miles, with the people's pride in themselves broken, they felt open and willing to try things they had never dreamed before.

From the beginning, Miles says he emphasized the spiritual dimension of church life. In his preaching he stresses members' need for a personal relationship with Jesus Christ as well as the need to be filled continuously with the Holy Spirit. He places the authority of Scripture front and center for practice as well as doctrine.

He vigorously attacked a prevailing attitude of "cheap grace" he had witnessed in many other city churches, and began discipling people in small groups. And frequent spiritual renewal events (such as a one-week retreat) helped transform the people's spiritual depth, joy, and love.

Miles makes an interesting observation about St. John's old-timers. He believes a powerful spiritual life existed within the church about 50 years ago. Those over 70 are spiritually-minded toward others and faithful worshipers; but, Miles wonders, what happened in the intervening generations?

Though at first the renewed spiritual emphasis resulted in only a handful of new people, the congregation clearly grew in increased love and faithfulness in worship. Visitors began to describe St. John's as "very loving" instead of "very cold."

In the mid-1980s worship attendance peaked at about 180 compared to 104 in 1980. Now the church enjoys another growth spurt, and today attendance averages about 250. About 50 percent of the growth comes through adult confirmation and the other 50 percent by accession from other denominations. In nine years, only one new family came "the easy way," by transfer from a sister church of someone moving to New York.

The congregation bases its structure on numerous cell groups for Bible study, growth and nurture, and outreach. Support groups for addictions and weight control, and youth and young singles groups also attract community members.

Was there tension? "Certainly," says Miles. About 20 people grew uncomfortable with the increased expectation for spiritual knowledge and commitment. They either transferred to another church or dropped out altogether. And some tension still remains. About half of today's members are enthusiastic about the changes, while the other half ranges from accepting to unsure.

St. John's vision? The members plan to enlarge their school, offices, and narthex. They intend to double Sunday attendance. Though land is too costly to expand the facilities, growth won't end—the congregation is already in the process of planting new churches.

Beyond their own spiritual growth, Miles and St. John's other staff anticipate increasing their ministry to people whose lives are broken by the modern American lifestyle. They want to touch people whose marriages and families are torn apart and who need delivery from various addictions.

Miles sums up: "I think you can be an inner-city church where nobody is building, nobody is moving in, where there is nothing— no demographic factors—that can be relied on for growth. The church can still grow."

Sometimes, being on the cutting edge of spiritual growth and change means courageously risking one's very ministry. Such was the case for Pastor Ingo Dutzmann at Redeemer Church of Cape Elizabeth, a suburb of Portland, ME. The people at Redeemer thought Dutzmann "came on like gangbusters." They had already declined to about 100 in worship—and the decline accelerated after his arrival, in spite of the fact that Maine (along with Nevada) has the highest percentage of unchurched people in the nation (70 percent).

He began his ministry on Aug. 1, 1983. By late the next month, he felt the need to call a congregational meeting on confessional integrity, that is, on how faithfully (or, in this case, faithlessly) the congregation was putting into practice its stated beliefs. The Lutheran Church—Missouri Synod (including Dutzmann) confesses, believes, teaches, and practices that when people receive Holy Communion together, they publicly witness to a unity in public doctrine. Therefore, their churches do not freely open their altar rails to just anybody but only to members of denominations in "altar and pulpit fellowship" with The Lutheran Church—Missouri Synod. Although Redeemer's constitution stated this position, the congregation didn't follow it. Dutzmann did.

During that congregational meeting, he tried at first to sidestep the question of what he would do if this issue was unresolved. Finally he said that if he could not in clear conscience serve there as a confessional Lutheran, he would have to leave. He also told the members they shouldn't apologize for this approach; being distinctively Lutheran is precisely what would attract outside people into membership. People are looking for ultimate answers, he said, and they will receive that at Redeemer.

Soon after, several top congregational leaders asked Dutzmann to leave—not only Redeemer but also the ministry. When he didn't, three families left the church because they thought it was becoming too conservative.

Dutzmann's commitment to spiritual growth doesn't end with adherence to the Lutheran Confessions' understanding of scriptural truth. He also emphasizes that prayer begin and end every enterprise (including cleaning day), and that confession and absolution be practiced in daily matters.

Dutzmann takes Bible study seriously. Several lay people received training in teaching Crossways material, and several others lead small-group Bible study.

Lay leaders help with Sunday services, especially when Dutzmann is out of town. Dutzmann taught his elders to use already prepared sermons and to add their own personal insights. He tries to offer each elder two preaching opportunities a year. He says, "Let's face it. Some of the things coming from the heart and well grounded in the Word can certainly be done by lay people."

Members carry involvement beyond church and Bible study. Dutzmann explains he offers everyone a job until they accept one God has suited for them. He finds out their strengths and frees them for service.

With a district church consultant's help, Redeemer developed a vision that includes starting both a Christian day school and a sister congregation, adding several more staff members (especially for youth and evangelism), and continuing building expansion.

Dutzmann describes himself as a "persuader" who isn't satisfied with the status quo. Obviously! His first career was serving as an administrator at Oakland University, Rochester, MI, overseeing a sizeable staff and budget. He had also been a lay leader at a 4,000-member congregation in MI. Clearly, he was equipped to be a leader for the congregation's spiritual growth.

In his six years at Redeemer, attendance grew from 78 to 204, Communion attendance doubled, Sunday school enrollment jumped from 21 to 114, and the budget increased from $46,000 to $125,000. He added two services a week and gave guidance to two building-expansion projects.

Looking back, Dutzmann says he would have started off differently by spending more time discovering and discerning the hopes, fears, and aspirations of congregational leaders, and that he would avoid his tendency to become confrontational when basic doctrine or his divine call was questioned or tested.

"I've learned that outward affects and concerns, modeled after our Lord's, can literally allow a strong antagonist to become more positive without feeling that he or she is being pushed, cajoled or manipulated," he says. "In fact, as contrary as it may sound, it's a fact that many who were once strong antagonists are now at the leading edge of the positive growth of the congregation. Praise God."

Offering Variety in Adult Education

These courageous churches also reflect this priority of Bible study by the kind and variety of studies they offer in any given week. The Rev. Theodore Eisold of Immanuel in Palatine, IL, reports there's almost always a Bible class going on at the church.

Some are what he calls "triple track" classes. Since many members travel extensively, they can sign up for a class at 6 a.m. on Monday. But, if they can't be there then, they can take the same class at 10 a.m. that morning or at 7:30 p.m. that evening.

"Adult education is really good for our congregation," Eisold concludes. "And it's extensive. We've even had seven-hour sessions in one day on various topics." Church members certainly catch the idea that Bible study takes priority.

The Rev. Bradley Hoefs of King of Kings in Omaha, NE, shares a story that epitomizes the creative way these courageous churches meet their unique people's needs through Bible study.

King of Kings effectively reaches baby boomers. "During Lent, we decided to offer a Wednesday night Bible class before worship services and run our weekday school at the same time. I taught a class called 'Emotional Wellness in the Scriptures.' They're really hungry for something like that. The first night we had 211 people!"

King of Kings recognizes that people live at different levels of spiritual maturity. The church presents classes for those who have studied the Bible for some time, and "we also try to be sensitive to the fact that we need to offer some things to those for whom this will be the first time participating in a Bible class," Hoefs asserts.

"They really need a nonthreatening environment."

Our Savior, Centereach, NY, is in a slow-growing suburb on Long Island. Founded in 1958, it experienced good growth through the 1960s, then began to decline in the 70s and early 80s. But this trend was reversed soon after The Rev. Ronald Stelzer's arrival in 1984, and church attendance doubled from 148 to 326 in five years.

In his assessment, Our Savior suffered from low morale after 10 difficult years. They had lost a popular pastor on the heels of a major building drive, and then suffered steady decline. Members were ready for new leadership and direction. "There weren't many ghosts to be fought," Stelzer sums up.

Stelzer emphasizes that people get into the Word of God and apply the Bible as God's inerrant Word. He notes that spiritual growth occurs when "I just start preaching and teaching the Word."

He taught a quickly growing adult class, now averaging 100 a week, on Sunday between two services. After developing a core of teachers in the Bethel Bible series and the Navigators' 2:7 series, teaching had even more impact. Wednesday evening became Christian education time, currently with six Bethel classes, three 2:7 classes, Stelzer's prospective members' class, an activity/music time for preteens, recreation and tutoring programs for high school and confirmation youth, and childcare for little ones—all running simultaneously. New members today believe that ongoing Bible study is Our Savior's norm.

Stelzer says he was not afraid to take a stand on controversial issues, and this initially raised tensions but ultimately raised the commitment level. He worked with church leaders to change the constitution to include a policy and procedure for church discipline. He spoke out against universalism, abortion, evolution, and homosexuality, and emphasized Biblical stewardship in terms of tithing. He affirms that only men could serve as elders, though women take leadership roles in all other aspects of ministry. "I have lost members because of these stands, and also lost prospective members when I emphasize there is no salvation apart from faith in Christ, but the general trend of the quantity and quality of commitment of those I gain and keep is up."

Stelzer believes that growth occurs with no sacrifice of essentials. The Great Commission continues as the church's mission statement and theme. "If you're interested in winning people to Christ and helping them grow in Christ—if that's your focus, it helps you make a lot of other decisions."

The foundation for growth in Trinity, Lisle, IL (a Chicago suburb), also came from the congregation's commitment to renewal through Bible study. Pastor Arthur Beyer's long pastorate gives perspective to recent growth. Ministering to a young, educated, multiethnic and multiracial neighborhood, Trinity's growth curve for attendance went from 511 in 1983 to 639 in 1988. Annual adult confirmations grew from 36 to 70 in that time.

Because managers and professionals in this community often move, Beyer outlasted most of the original leaders. The positive side of turnover is that few firmly held traditions worry the members. The pastor describes the congregation as open to and positive about change.

After coming close to a split in the early 1970s, members discovered that not even the church officers were studying the Bible. Today, Trinity's hallmark is Bible study. Its goal? That members understand that growth in the Word is the norm for all adults in order to be equipped for mission. To emphasize that norm, no one may serve in the congregation in any fashion unless they take part in a Bible study. Leaders must also participate in a "Center for Leadership Development" offered on Sunday mornings and during the week.

New members join a three-year curriculum, also offered on Sunday morning. These basic classes are well attended due to a constant flow of new members. Study continues through "electives" offered every day except Friday. The director of Christian education, Dr. Jack Giles, with a doctorate in educational administration of adult education, has supervised these well-developed programs for eight years.

In Milpitas, CA, Pastor Michael Gibson of Mount Olive learned the need for patience. "If I had tried three years ago to do what we're doing now, I would have blown the church apart. We concentrated on guiding and spiritually nurturing a core group, and we grew together in knowing our purpose and method.

"It's significant that we could take a church that has been in existence for 29 years and turn it around and do what some of my colleagues think is rather radical. All that and not blow up the church in the process!"

De Witt, IA, a small town of 4,300 near the Mississippi River and 20 miles north of Davenport, is stable in population. Grace Church was founded there in 1925. In 1982 the pastor and 200-some members left to form another congregation. Right after the split, worship averaged about 280 and baptized membership was 750. Pastor Ronald Goodsman came to Grace in early 1983. By 1991 membership totaled 1400.

A veteran pastor, Goodsman had rebuilt two other congregations. He firmly believes a congregation should be able to say of its pastor, "In matters of doctrine our pastor stands like a rock, and in all other matters he's the most accommodating and loving person I know."

Using Small Groups

Many of the churches we studied report active involvement in small-group ministry, most commonly in home Bible study groups. These small groups serve the church's ministry in two ways. First, they provide an infrastructure for congregations in which people can interact, grow in their prayer life together, meet fellowship needs, and study the Bible in depth. Second, they serve as an avenue for outreach, especially when placed strategically throughout the community.

When Pastor Roland Kauth of Zion arrived in Fairbanks, AK, establishing small groups was one of the things he emphasized. Now "we have a number of cottage Bible studies. We have a couple going at the church, plus those out in the neighborhood. This is one area where I feel God has richly blessed the study of the Word and brought people into contact with us through it."

The small-group approach provides a subtle shift in the way people approach Bible study, and it provides dramatic results. Many Christians grew up with an understanding that the pastor, the professional, or a few key leaders must paternalistically guard the truth. Only these well-trained professionals could feed the truth to the flock, usually through lecture. This paternalistic role encouraged a passive view toward Scripture, a view in which church members primarily perceive themselves as receivers. No wonder 'Bible study' drew few participants!

The churches in our study have, in a sense, indigenized the

65

Gospel by placing it in lay people's hands. In this way, these congregations truly represent the spirit of the Reformation. They're equipping and releasing congregational members to study and grow in the Word on their own. At first, this approach appears to threaten the pastor's authority. But none of the pastors we interviewed reported any problems.

Pastor Michael Gibson explains how Mount Olive in Milpitas, CA, equips its people for Bible study. "We show our people how to do a half-dozen different types of Bible studies to make a difference in their own faith walk. We have a long-term goal of developing 'discipleship groups.' That's the kind of group where one individual meets with another and then that person meets with another. It's a Paul and Timothy kind of thing. We introduce them to different study tools, including references that they can purchase. We give them a listing of reasonably priced books that they can use as a home Bible study library. We teach them how to do a biographical study. We show them how to be involved in various disciplines, including word study, cross-references and how to use their study Bibles."

Some courageous churches activate small-group ministries on a short-term basis. This happens at Our Savior in Centereach, NY. "During the summers, we have small groups that meet for short four- to six-week courses," the Rev. Ronald Stelzer explains. Stelzer notes that people consider the experience positive and often want to continue them. "Small groups are starting to develop because the people just can't get enough," he says. "So they want to get together. One of my challenges is to make sure that we're growing in a healthy, systematic way toward using small groups."

Churches in our sample report that small group ministries provide an excellent environment for ministry among members as well as for outreach. They encourage prayer life, care-giving, assimilation of new members, and mutual edification within the body. This relational aspect of ministry is something difficult to duplicate in a formal worship setting. In small groups, people grow together as they grow spiritually in the Word.

Pastor Ronald Zehnder of St. Luke in Ann Arbor, MI, indicates that 28 small, weekly or biweekly Bible study groups in that church involve about 280 people. "They've been very significant in the life of our church because a lot of ministry takes place there," says

Zehnder. "They're designed around five prongs: worship, study, fellowship, witnessing, and service projects."

Pastor Christopher Dodge at Walled Lake, MI, tells how God has blessed St. Matthew's small group ministry. "We have a fairly large number of individuals who are in home Bible studies," says Dodge. "People have developed friends in those Bible studies. A lot of new people meet others there, and I think that has had a major impact in our church. People are beginning to look at what the Word has to say about their personal lifestyles and what it means to be followers of Christ."

Charlotte, MI, a small town 20 miles from Lansing, hopes for growth soon, although average-to-slow growth has been normal for the town. First Church, founded in 1949, experienced major internal tensions in the late 1960s and 70s and watched its baptized membership decrease from 365 to 230. In the late 1970s, Pastor Gary Doroh brought healing and strengthened the congregation's spiritual foundation.

The current pastor, the Rev. Paul Moldenhauer, came in 1981 from the seminary. He says that the church's soil was fertile and that God's Word and Sacrament ministry bore abundant fruit during the 1980s, when membership rose to 564 and average worship attendance grew from 64 in 1974 to 243 in 1990. Moldenhauer offers a strong biblical reason why cell-group ministry plays such a powerful role in the church. "My dad is a pastor, and he always told me, 'Get your people into the Word, and the Lord will take care of the rest of it.' I think it's absolutely true—the power is in the Word."

"We definitely see that as very critical to the vibrancy of our congregation. There's so much that happens through those home Bible studies in terms of ministry among members. That's the body of Christ at work. It doesn't necessitate me having to visit all these people. They're visiting each other. They're ministering to each other by praying for each other in those home Bible studies."

Prince of Peace, Carrollton, TX, builds programs around action. Adult Bible study, especially on Sunday, shifted from mostly information-based exchange to training for a ministry. Small groups number about 30. The staff carefully identifies small group leaders, teaches them how to care for those in the group as well as others outside, and encourages them to reach out, to incorporate new people in their group and then multiply by division.

Preparing, Praising, and Petitioning

Prayer, in various forms, stands as another mighty ingredient of the courageous churches in our sample.

"It takes courage. Dare I pray for this growth?" asks Dr. Paul Meyer in Orange, CA, reflecting on the growth he experiences in ministry at Salem. "Both my prayer life for courage and my strength has increased. So also has my praise life for the Lord's ministry in the life of our 'saints of Salem.' "

Prayer also prepares people for change. Pastor Henry Biar in San Antonio, TX, says that when he came, 50 people worshiped on Sunday morning. After receiving some outreach training, he discussed those principles with his leaders. They recognized that both numerical and spiritual growth was imperative at King of Kings.

Though their church participated in church growth training events, Biar summarizes the transition by underscoring the importance of prayer. "All of this was guided by the fact that we went to the Lord in prayer during worship services and through personal prayer time. We were always seeking His direction and support."

Pastor John Frerking of Faith in North Palm Beach, FL, saw prayer as part of the mix that helped make his church effective, as well as contributed to his personal life. "Effective ministry means constant change. And constant change that is meaningful and worthwhile involves constant research, constant evaluation, consistent leadership, and continual prayer." Frerking adds that the process of change demonstrated to him the need for a pastor to "spend time in study, prayer, reading, and leisure."

In a number of these congregations, prayer plays an important role in public worship. Pastor Warren Arndt of Faith in Troy, MI, says he invites people forward to pray with him at the end of every service; he no longer goes to the door to greet people as they leave. "I welcome visitors and guests up front. Anyone who wants prayer can also come forward, for whatever needs they might have." Both Arndt and lay ministers stand at the altar. "We have people coming up in all of our services just for prayer—sometimes as many as 200." (Faith's prayer time includes a "prayer and praise report." During the week, people fill out reports—including prayer requests, petitions, and reasons for thanksgiving—and place them in prayer boxes in the narthex.)

Many churches speak dramatically about the spiritual warfare they face within the congregation and mention prayer's importance in that context. The response of prayer to situations that exceed human capabilities and resources indicates that God is breaking down both pride and despair, natural human reactions. Instead of depending upon themselves or giving up, congregations that turn around are congregations that pray.

When the late Rev. Dennis Schiefelbein arrived at Our Savior in Corpus Christi, TX, a church that had been without a pastor for two years, he found the congregation "pretty much disintegrated. The Lord just pulled out all the crutches and drove me to my knees."

Prayer played an important role as the church began to grow. "The biggest change which has occurred, of course, is spiritual. The congregation went from being spiritually exhausted to spiritually renewed. The spiritual renewal took place as more people were also driven to their knees. The church just started to pray. I really think that prayer is the thing that turned the church around. And it continues to be."

Schiefelbein touched on a subject prevalent among North American leaders—enlisting prayer supporters. "I had to surround myself with prayer partners. I believe every pastor certainly has to surround himself with people upholding him in prayer, standing by him shoulder to shoulder in prayer. If Satan is going to get after him, he's going to have to go through those people."

Schiefelbein said scriptural teaching on prayer greatly influenced his ministry. He identified those with the gift of intercession, and he activated those intercessors to pray for the ministry. And he took his own teachings to heart. "I get up and pray for two hours, between 5 and 7 a.m. A lot of my battles and a lot of frustrations are worked through at that time."

In Schiefelbein's first year, little happened in the church. He tried to get old members to reach out, but not one new member came to faith. Finally he asked himself how he would start a new church if he had nothing. Here at least he had a building, worship, some classes, and a modest program. He was already ahead. Now he just had to go out and start evangelizing and not wait for the rest of the church to come along.

What happened, Schiefelbein explained, is that a new church developed right under the noses of the older members. The new people became leaders and brought their friends and relatives into church. Growth took off. Schiefelbein believed it was crucial to find new leaders not locked into traditional thinking.

Our Savior expected great commitment from its people. Every member is expected to be in church and Bible study each Sunday. New people aren't allowed to join until they sign up for a Sunday morning class. The children of people who have been members for more than a year must attend Sunday school regularly for a year before they are allowed to begin attending a class in preparation for first Communion or the rite of confirmation. If people do not want to study God's Word, Schiefelbein suggested they join a different church.

The congregation's spiritual life was vibrant. Many church members held prayer lunches. Male headship in spiritual matters grew in the church and in families. A men's prayer group regularly met to stand in prayer against Satan's attacks of church families. Soon, a prayer coordinator, a woman moving from NE, will lead this specialized ministry. She prays three to six hours a day. Our Savior hopes to begin a 24-hour-a-day prayer line, encouraging anyone in Corpus Christi to call at any time for someone to pray for them. A new prayer chapel will stress prayer around the clock.

Worship styles varied at the church. On Communion Sunday, the service was more liturgical, including chanting in a lively but traditional way. Other Sundays followed a free-form style. On those Sundays, the service frequently began without Schiefelbein. A band of guitars, basses, and some singers started the worship with song. Soon afterward, Schiefelbein offered the prayers of the day. People made their prayer requests at several podiums around the church. The prayer of the day could be lengthy; sometimes requests ran two pages long.

After worship, Schiefelbein usually stayed in front to pray with people who came forward for special prayer. "I figure that prayer for and with my people is more important than greeting my people," he explained. Sometimes prayer continued an hour-and-a-half after worship ended.

The congregation recently risked relocating to a new site. The parent denomination's "Laborers for Christ," a group of volunteer retirees from around the nation with construction experience, built a multipurpose room. Our Savior members prayed they would double in size in the next two years.

The church no longer receives subsidy from the denomination and contributes $20,000 of its offerings to missions. Making the financial commitment to relocate and simultaneously to go off subsidy was a courageous step.

What has he learned? Schiefelbein answered, "I would have gotten down to the work of 'praying in the harvest' a whole lot faster. I would have less fear about rocking boats and knocking heads with tradition than I did my first few years. But once the Lord got hold of me and forced me to my knees, He's been setting a good pace of growth and change and has opened doors at every junction. One of the biggest things I've learned is that Jesus must be absolute Lord of His church. I've also learned not to take myself so seriously, to enjoy the ride every day."

Praying for the Pastor

Experience with his staff-led, high-expectation ministry taught also the Rev. Steve Wagner of Prince of Peace, Carrollton, TX, the importance of having a small support group for himself. "My support group has been together about 10 years. My commitment to them is that they can ask me anything they want about my life, my family, and my savings account—and they have complete access to my *Daytimer,* so they know how I spend my time. I take to them issues of ministry, knowing that anything I share is completely confidential. Those guys are as close friends as I will have in this world. They support me and want the ministry to work and work well. You just grow and mature in this kind of accountability structure," Wagner notes. "Now I'm sensing the need for these groups to take on extended periods of praying for one another. I look forward to that."

Searching for Spiritual Gifts

Spiritual gifts constitute a way of life and thinking for pastors, leaders, and most members of courageous churches. The scriptural teaching on spiritual gifts encourages members' ministry within congregations, providing an atmosphere of vitality and growth. As a rule, courageous churches help their members to discover their spiritual gifts and to develop and use them as as means for living out the priesthood of all believers.

The Rev. Terry Tieman of Bethel in Fort Smith, AR, says, "It was an important decision for our congregation to enter the Two-Year Church Growth Process. That decision led to the practice of using spiritual gifts in the process of selecting leaders and filling service positions. This helped invigorate the leadership of our congregation by providing new blood as well as taking the burden of work off a few people and spreading it to the many."

Many churches in our study do what Tieman does: introduce spiritual gifts as part of a new members' class. "Whenever we have a new members class, we usually spend the last period taking the people through a spiritual gifts inventory. They fill that out, and then we try to get back to them with a suggested list of ministries they can become involved in, based on their spiritual gifts. We also have a spiritual gifts director. I really think that people are beginning to understand that each one of them has gifts they can use to serve God in a particular way."

St. Mark Church in Kentwood, MI, also sees the importance of spiritual gifts says the Rev. Rodney Otto. The church celebrates a spiritual gifts Sunday each year.

Pastor Wagner at Prince of Peace, Carrollton, TX, uses a more sophisticated way to keep track of the spiritual gifts ministry in his congregation: keeping the "spiritual gift mix" on a computer.

Perhaps the Rev. Theodore Hartman of St. John's, Bakersfield, CA, sums it up best. "The Lord has been at work here using the gifts of His people. I've grown more confident and assertive in the use of my personal gifts and abilities and have become far less critical of my own lack of gifts in some areas. That allows me to go to my strengths and to encourage and depend on the strengths of others. It has also caused me to raise my sights in the kingdom and remove the self-imposed limiters of what I thought possible."

Perspective

Most of the techniques in this chapter are common-sense ways to present the ministry, identify audiences, clarify presentations, treat guests well, and follow up carefully.

Wise pastors and leaders recognize and rely on the fundamental truth that the Holy Spirit calls and gathers a congregation. The best way to be healthy in the Lord is to tap into the Holy Spirit's power and to cultivate His movement. This means centering on the Word and Sacrament through which Jesus Christ gives Himself. Public worship, of course, does this. Yet Christians expose themselves to even more of God's power when they supplement public worship with Bible study in which they have opportunity to interact with the text and with each other and discover applications of the Word for themselves.

Prayer keeps people dependent on God's will and guidance— just as Jesus prayed in the Garden, "Yet not My will, but Yours be done."

The churches we interviewed clearly report how important it is for them to personally interact with God through Bible study and Scripture-centered prayer.

That's why Pastor Gibson at Mount Olive tries to pray lavishly in every activity to keep a spiritual base evident.

That's why Pastor Stelzer and Our Savior's leaders work hard to make group Bible studies the norm for church life.

That's why Trinity's leaders require formal Bible study as a prerequisite to leadership.

And that's why Pastor Schiefelbein and Our Savior leaders took the forceful stand of suggesting that anybody not wanting to study God's Word attend another church.

The churches in this study keep their sights on the fundamental goal: bringing people into spiritual life with Jesus Christ. To repeat Pastor Ron Stelzer's comment, "If you're interested in winning people to Christ and helping them grow in Christ . . . if that's your focus, it helps you make a lot of other decisions."

To repeat the spiritual-growth principles presented in chapter 1:

- Church leaders consider Bible study as key to growth. They understand that churches grow because people are growing spiritually through the Word of God.

- They stress small-group ministries that include prayer and spiritual growth.

- Prayer takes high priority in the pastor's and church leaders' lives and is reflected in the churches' corporate lifestyle, which includes prayer lists, prayer services, and prayer chains. Courageous congregations understand the reality of Satan's attacks and the need to prepare for spiritual warfare.

- Most church leaders teach the concept of spiritual gifts and help members to discover, develop, and use their gift. Spiritual gifts serve as the criteria for deploying people into *ministry opportunities* rather than just into offices, boards, titles, or committees. These churches often assimilate new members through some type of spiritual gifts' discovery process.

Chapter 4

Celebrative Worship: The Drawing Power of Christ

Yet a time is coming and has now come when the true worshipers will worship the Father in spirit and truth, for they are the kind of worshipers the Father seeks. God is spirit, and His worshipers must worship in spirit and in truth.

John 4:23–24

Worship is the tip of the iceberg, the most visible part of a congregation's ministry, the most apparent expression of a congregation's doctrinal depth, breadth and weight, as well as its mission-minded attitude. The courageous churches in this report frequently discuss it; many had deliberately changed their worship forms in order to make them relevant to members as well as easily followed by visitors.

Growing churches are visitor sensitive. Members welcome strangers and help them to feel at home. Their friendly outreach view provides for visitor parking, printed worship services that are easily followed, and other tools that aid in making visitors feel welcome and part of the worshiping body.

Celebrating in New Ways

These courageous churches, pointed toward outreach and growth, made significant changes in worship. At Our Savior, Corpus Christi, TX, "We no longer use a hymnal, but print a worship bulletin each Sunday," said the late Rev. Dennis Schiefelbein. Our Savior adopted a new liturgy for Communion Sundays and offers nonliturgical services on non-Communion Sundays.

"People follow along in their Bibles during the preaching and reading of the Word. Many take notes," Schiefelbein added. He used an expository style of preaching, and in the non-Communion services he provided eight opportunities for prayer. Our Savior also offered an excellent children's church program for three- to five-year-olds during both Sunday morning services.

"We've attempted to make the worship services warm, enthusiastic, personal, and practical," Schiefelbein summed up. "Yet our worship services are dignified. We've attempted to structure our services so the first-time visitor with limited worship experience will never get lost and will be edified by the experience."

Immanuel in Palatine, IL, developed innovative approaches in its effort to reach younger people. The church, founded in 1869 in one of Chicago's outer suburbs, is now experiencing rapid growth.

In 1988, demonstrating that unconventional solutions work, the Rev. Robert Clausen, senior pastor since 1976, chose to be relieved of administrative leadership and become associate to a new senior pastor, the Rev. Theodore Eisold. The arrangement works well.

In the late 1970s Immanuel's growth stagnated. Meanwhile its leaders watched the phenomenal growth of Willow Creek Community Church in nearby South Barrington, whose worship services attract 11,000 today. The potential for courageous growth in Palatine was obvious.

Clausen saw a need to develop a Sunday worship experience attractive to people with a different Christian background. He and some lay leaders flew to the West Coast to observe other well-known Christian churches.

Calling on his previous experience in evangelistic outreach and in teaching drama at a church school, Clausen developed "The Good News Hour" as an alternative worship service. The church views this service as a constantly evolving experiment.

Each "Good News Hour" service is custom designed, but they all follow a basic outline. The service begins with a word of welcome, music, opening hymns, a brief litany of praise and some Scripture readings interspersed with various hymns. Often the choir sings three or four selections. The sermon usually comes last, just before the benediction (although its position changes on Sundays when Communion is offered). The pastors work diligently to keep the service scriptural and theologically strong.

This format is used in two of the four services each weekend. The other two services are traditional, using *The Lutheran Hymnal,* and meet the needs of a segment of the congregation. However, the two contemporary services outdraw the two traditional ones by three to one. Clausen and Eisold consider "The Good News Hour" to be one of the finest contemporary services in the Lutheran church. More importantly, they feel Immanuel is touching a responsive nerve.

Immanuel's leaders aim for 1,000 worshipers every Sunday, but not at any cost—and surely not at the cost of their church's doctrinal heritage. They know they must fuse together many factors and must fight discouragement when some efforts fail. Yet they keep trying, believing that many other congregations can imitate Immanuel's efforts.

Pastor Michael Gibson of Mount Olive, Milpitas, CA, recalls the congregation's struggle to reach people. "We've tried to design our worship in such a way that it is, to use the term of Silicon Valley, where we're located, user friendly. That's made a huge difference. For many people, their first introduction to church is on Sunday morning. We've tried to preach practical messages. Obviously, we communicate the truth of Scripture; but we do so with primary emphasis on what difference it makes for the individual today. Then we move on toward leading people to Christ.

"We look at our worship services as a means to the end of bringing people to Christ rather than an end in itself," explains Gibson. "We try to involve our lay people a great deal. We have an elder who welcomes everyone and explains that the worship service is printed in the bulletin. Then we have a Time of Praise, using contemporary praise songs with lyrics that frequently are right out of Scripture. The elder encourages people to turn and greet everyone. It's a lot of fun to start worship that way. I preach the message in an expository style. There's an outline in the bulletin every Sunday. We've found that preaching a series of sermons also works very well and keeps people coming back."

To keep our balance on the subject, we need to point out that extremely contemporary worship services may be unneeded, in some settings. In fact, for Redeemer, Stuart, FL, retaining the traditional service is preferable. Founded in 1958, the congregation lies on the northern edge of the population explosion in southeast

Florida, 30 miles north of Palm Beach. In 10 years, baptized membership grew from 400 to 1,400. The present head pastor, the Rev. Dean Pingel, notes that much of the church's growth is attributable to people who move in from the Midwest and Northeast, many from Lutheran backgrounds. "Our people have a good sense of what Lutheran worship is. On a continuum from low church to high church, we're certainly past the halfway point towards the high-church side."

Combining Contemporary and Traditional

Many of these courageous churches did not abandon traditional worship styles altogether. Many retain at least some traditional services. Some, like Faith in North Palm Beach, FL, offer both each week. Pastor John Frerking describes Faith's worship as visitor friendly but basically traditional. However, on Wednesday evenings, they provide an informal, laymen-led worship service that does not use the hymnal. Frerking explains, "I don't do anything in that service except celebrate the Sacrament. I stay in the background. The lay people choose the Scripture readings and lead the discussion. For music, we use synthesizers and guitars. It's very laid back; they do a good job."

Dr. Paul W. Meyer of Salem, Orange, CA, says of himself, "I'm a church historian at heart, and all those old forms are near and dear to me. I love masses and the litanies. But I have had to learn to accommodate the worship needs of our people. My worship planning has evolved, trying to grapple with the very, very serious problem of how to communicate with and to new Christians." He continues to use the denominational hymnal but has added three other song books as well as a core of young musicians who lead "pre-songs" to begin each service; and they also have started to do things during Communion. "Sometimes the old-timers don't like it, but there aren't many old-timers any more."

Pastor Ronald Goodsman, at Grace, De Witt, IA, came to the congregation in 1983, right after a split in 1982. Goodsman thought it important to keep worship as traditional as possible at Grace, since their worship life grew somewhat chaotic during their struggles. Unopened copies of a new hymnal were in boxes when he arrived, but Goodsman ignored them. Finally, at a voter's meeting, a member asked him what he thought about the new hymnal. He said, "The service belongs to the congregation. Whatever the congregation decides to do [about which hymnal to use], I'm very content with, and I'm your servant. A change has to come from the congregation because it will not come from your pastor.' They broke out into great applause." However, in 1989, attendance jumped 13 percent when Grace added a third, more contemporary worship service. Goodsman claims he's doing everything that shouldn't work. He still uses the King James lectionary with the one year series, and the liturgy right from the old *Lutheran Hymnal.*

St. John, Glendale, NY, departs from the traditional style of worship on Wednesday evenings during Lent. Because the change was so positively received the church has continued Wednesday evening services every week. Pastor Donald Miles tells how the service evolved:

"I guess it was about four or five years ago, during Lent. I just got tired of all the depression during those weeks. I got tired of all that gloomy, horrible music and no hallelujahs. I said to myself, 'I can't do it anymore.'

"We resolved that we were going to bring in our contemporary music ministry group for Wednesday night Lenten services. We decided that we would praise the Lord with all our hearts. We did! We praised, we clapped, and sang and rejoiced and 'hallelujahed.' It was one of the most lively, joyful Lenten seasons that I'd ever seen anywhere. And people had so much fun with that! They loved it. They were so blessed by it that we just continued after Easter."

Shepherd of the Hills in Onalaska, WI, describes itself as semi-traditional. "Our worship experiences focus on involving the worshipers in as many ways as possible," says Pastor Barrie Henke. "We don't follow the strict liturgical forms but try to be flexible in the structures while maintaining our unique Lutheran integrity. We attempt to make a comfortable worship environment which is meaningful.

"We always have a printed folder and try to get away from a lot of flipping through the hymnal. That turns people off, especially those who are visiting for the first time and who are totally unfamiliar with a hymnal." Shepherd of the Hills also offers an informal Monday night service.

Pastor John Miller in Humble, TX, says "Worship needs to be

an exciting time that lifts people to God." Lamb of God Church also offers Holy Communion in each service and prints out the service in a worship folder.

Pastor Raymond Cummings in Walden, NY, cites the Charismatic Renewal Movement as profoundly impacting his congregation's worship. "Charismatic renewal provided for us more joy and friendliness in worship," he says.

Trinity did not replace a liturgical worship form with a contemporary, but provides a mixture instead. "We follow a traditional style but use contemporary worship songs, and we give opportunity for people to give testimonies. We also offer a Sunday evening service of prayer and praise."

While quite conservative in doctrine and application of the Word, the Rev. Ronald Stelzer of Our Savior, Centereach, NY, is very open in church lifestyle. He says, "I'm not a rigid, one-way Lutheran in style. I don't believe we're called to be a 16th-century clone from Germany. I'm discouraged when churches try to be that and then wonder why they're not accomplishing something and criticize everyone else who is." The church's Sunday worship, open and flexible, varies from traditional to contemporary and from highly formal to quite informal. Both services offer the same service each Sunday, but one Sunday varies from another. Stelzer makes use of three different hymnals and songbooks to develop special formats occasionally. A range of instruments, suitable to the style and occasion, provide music.

"I try not to shake anybody up too much," says Stelzer. "So when I make a change, I do just a little here and a little there. I make it comfortable for them and condition them to be flexible. I don't think anybody has complained about our worship styles in the past three years."

Pastor Paul Moldenhauer of First Church, Charlotte, MI, says, "You have to have a worship style that will fit the needs of those people, and we just happen to have a lot of people that could go either way. It's very important that worship be friendly, need-meeting, exciting, celebrative, and that it have a message people can take home."

Adding Worship Opportunities

Christ in Southwick, MA, became outreach oriented and moved from one to four worship services. Pastor Jeffrey King feels that multiple services brought about quantity growth. "We have a variety of worship opportunities, and each is uniquely designed with a particular audience in mind." The four services include a 9 a.m. contemporary worship celebration—fast-paced, uplifting and committed to musical excellence—which is the most popular. A traditional service from the hymnal marks the 10:30 am. service. A half-hour informal Thursday evening service entitled "Quiet Moments for Busy People" is immediately followed by adult seminars. A Monday evening Jamaican service, offered from May until September, reaches migrant farm workers in the area.

Crafting Unique Weekly Worship

Many of these courageous churches provide a variety of worship services so that each Sunday differs greatly from another. Pastor Thomas Teske shapes the worship services at King of Kings in Arvada, CO, in this way: "We have the same worship in both services on Sunday, but no two Sundays are alike," he says. "I'm convinced that our worship is one of the most important evangelistic tools we have. That's not why we worship, but it's a by-product. I think that a church like ours, where the focus is on reaching out to new people, has to adapt its worship life accordingly. There's always variety in our services," Teske says. "We open our services every Sunday with a medley of several contemporary songs. Once a month we have folk services with guitars and other instruments, and we're moving in the direction of doing more of that in each service. At most services, we now have a 'worship team' at microphones leading the congregational songs and liturgy."

Though their service follows the liturgy, Teske uses about a third to two-thirds of the order of service in the *Lutheran Book of Worship* and fills in with other materials. "More and more, I spend more time on worship planning than I do on sermon writing, and I think that's the proper perspective. Worship is what the people are involved in. Visitors can feel comfortable and included here."

At Prince of Peace in Carrollton, TX, pastors Stephen Wagner and Paul Liersemann also take sections of the liturgy from the traditional hymnal and rewrite different parts each week. They focus on the Sacrament and message to make them "twin mountaintop experiences."

"We commune each Sunday in each of our three services," says Wagner. (This offering of the Sacrament in each service is a trend among many of these churches.) Two Sunday morning services are more traditional and liturgical, while the contemporary middle one involves an orchestra. The middle service "is almost exclusively contemporary, with praise-type music and new hymnody. It's designed to reach the younger adult and baby-boomer crowd."

Including Lay People

Pastor Tom Teske, Arvada, CO (introduced in the previous section), says his congregation's worship life also includes a great deal of lay participation in the worship and its administration. Besides greeting visitors, they come up front to welcome people and to make announcements. They read Scripture, offer prayers, and occasionally do the children's message. A recent banquet for worship assistants exceeded 100.

At Epiphany in Chandler, AZ, Pastor Larry Stoterau designs worship to be more relaxed and to involve many lay people. "Worship is conscientiously designed to include rather than exclude those to whom Lutheran worship may be unfamiliar. So members are good about inviting new neighbors and friends," explains Stoterau.

"We print out the worship service about 90 percent of the time when we're not using the hymnal. I begin the service in my suit, walking around the church. I'll try to identify visitors who are there for the first time and introduce myself to them. I'll also recognize some people who have been sick or who have been away and are back in church. It's much more relaxed. The service is a positive experience, and people are willing to come back. They say, 'I really enjoyed being here.'

"We have women very much involved in all parts of our service, except Communion. In addition to reading the lessons, laity write all the prayers for Sunday morning. For our ushering staff, we use whole families. We have ushers that may be 5 years old, and some might be 80 years old. But the whole family ushers—Mom, Dad, and the kids."

Tapping the Power of Friendliness

Friendliness presumes a worldview that reaches out. Pastor Jon Reusch at Hope, Warren, MI, says that after a denominational stewardship program that encouraged friendliness, "Our people underwent a gradual change of attitude toward God, fellow members, and those outside the fellowship of believers. We developed a spirit of acceptance, love, and joyful caring."

At nearby Immanuel at Mount Clemens, Pastor Michael Lutz sees visitors return in direct proportion to the congregation's friendliness. "Individuals are willing to reach out, and the desire they have to share the Lord is apparent. When individuals worship with us for the first time, they return."

The staff at King of Kings, Omaha, NE, consciously projects friendliness, which members are "catching." Pastor Bradley Hoefs explains, "We've committed ourselves to growing in friendliness, to become the friendliest church in our city. Our greeters not only greet people on the way in, but they look for visitors on the way out." (Visitors wear blue name tags; members, red.) "And, we work hard at allowing our people to fellowship and talk with one another. Probably, most significantly, we on the staff model it as much as possible."

In the strongly Jewish community of Beverly Hills, CA, the Rev. R. John Perling reports that the people of Mount Calvary challenged themselves to become a friendly church. "Our church has grown from a closed, exclusive group to an outreaching, loving, expanding, sharing, concerned band of followers of Messiah-Jesus."

The people at Bethel in Fort Smith, AR, today view visitors with new eyes: "We've always been perceived as a friendly church," says Pastor Terry Tieman. "But now it's more than, 'We're glad you're here and filling the space.' We now see each visitor as a person who may not know Jesus as their Savior, and who may not be in the kingdom. Now we ask the question, 'What can I do to facilitate that person coming into the kingdom?' "

Churches promote friendliness in many ways. At Our Savior in Centereach, NY, coffee and pastries between worship services encourage adults to sit at tables and relax. The pastor uses this setting to teach the Bible class.

Zion in Fairbanks, AK, works hard to establish relationships. Members' photographs hang on a picture board. Someone takes a picture of anyone visiting for two or three Sundays and adds it to the board. Nametags also help members to know one another.

Pastor Thomas Braun, of Family of Christ in Andover, MN, says one reason he believes his members are friendly is because 50 percent come from different Christian backgrounds. Braun implies that since people don't come from the same background, they're curious about each other and assimilate new people into congregational life.

The Rev. Ronald Kudick, pastor of Atonement in Glendale, AZ, says his church wasn't as friendly as they thought. "In the beginning, our mission had a problem," he recalls. "We assumed we were friendly. Then one visiting family indicated, very frankly, that we weren't friendly at all. Shaking hands and saying 'hello' isn't what some people consider to be a friendly church. So we decided we'd have to learn to greet people properly. We now work carefully with greeters, training them. We have meetings every year, and we contact certain people to take part in that ministry."

At Cross of Christ in Chattanooga, TN, Pastor Edwin Doepel takes greeting a step further—into the parking lot! "One of my trademarks is that I stand out in the parking lot every Sunday morning. We also have a team of 'minglers' that are in the parking lot every Sunday morning as well. I visited another church some distance from here last Sunday. I met a lady who had been to our church some time ago. She said, 'I remember your church. You were standing out in front of your church in a big white robe.' That turned out to be kind of a billboard that people see when they drive by."

Viewing Everything with a Visitor's Eye

Friendliness and a desire for outreach have led these courageous congregations to a number of unique ministries that provide a visitor-friendly atmosphere on Sunday mornings.

Many courageous churches, like Community Church in Flat Rock, MI, say the development of visitor-friendly or user-friendly worship styles results in quantity growth. This visitor sensitivity expresses itself in many ways.

For example, Pastor J. Arthur Cox of Grace, Bradford, PA, says, "The most important person on Sunday morning in our church is the visitor."

Pastor John H. Miller learned that it doesn't do much good to aggressively seek out and invite prospects to worship if the congregation doesn't truly welcome them or offer attractive programs. Worship must be an exciting experience that lifts the faith of people through God's promises.

At Lamb of God, Humble, TX, the worship service seldom exceeds an hour, and always includes Communion. Though the church preserves essential factors, it tries to make every service easy to follow and fresh, in order to maintain high interest. Surveys show that people appreciate the preaching and Communion most.

Tallmadge Church in Tallmadge, OH, knows that about 50 percent of the people who visit their congregation come from different Christian backgrounds. Pastor Glenn Brauer says, "We need to be sensitive to the needs of those people who visit us. We can't allow our service to be confusing to them."

At Holy Cross, Riverdale, GA, visitor sensitivity led to adding a new staff member. Because of the increasing number of Laotian refugees moving into their area, the church tries to make them feel welcome, respected, and needed. "We encouraged a gifted Laotian Christian, Khamphevy Minnicha, to become involved in the work of the congregation and gave him the respect and support to do the ministry," says the Rev. Ronald Jannsen. "He's now training to become a pastor, the first of his ethnic group in the denomination."

About 50 visitors come to Shepherd of the Hills, Rancho Cucamonga, CA, each Sunday. Pastor Elmer Thyr considers first-time visitors' worship experience to be critical. He wants them to feel uplifted, encouraged, inspired, and welcomed. Everything that's done—the building's appearance, music, message (not a "sermon"!), and interaction with others—must demonstrate quality. "In my opinion," Thyr says, "one reason so few churches are growing is that once people get in there, they're bored to tears or ashamed. People need to feel that a church is a happy, joyful place where something exciting is happening, where they'd be blessed if they hooked up with it."

Thyr observes that most unchurched people are attracted first of all by the preacher's message and personality, and secondly by musical beauty and their emotional response to it. Speaking understandably to the unchurched is Thyr's passion. He spends nearly a day and a half preparing the liturgy for the Sunday contemporary service. He wants to motivate and inspire, rather than educate, from the pulpit. Believing that education is better done in Bible classes, the congregation offers 12 classes. Their theme is "Bible Study—Seven Days a Week and Twice on Somedays." (Thyr places a high priority on offering people choice in programming and scheduling, and offers five services at Christmas and Easter.)

Making the Hymnal "User Friendly"

Sensitivity to visitors brings change, though not always a change in worship style, to these courageous congregations. The worship service at Good Shepherd in Collinsville, IL, is simple, traditional, and reverent, says Pastor Dennis Kastens. Since so many unchurched come from a Roman Catholic background, they identify with and appreciate this style—including the fact that the services never, for any reason extend beyond an hour.

St. John in Lawton, OK, also provides a traditional, visitor-sensitive service from the denominational hymnbook. Pastor Richard Mayer reports that, in addition, the church provides visitor parking, greeters, and name tags.

Pastor Ingo Dutzmann of Cape Elizabeth, ME, uses the hymnal but makes it more user friendly. "We realize the hymnal is difficult. It's difficult for members, let alone nonmembers. So we print out every section of every service, and we tell people on what page that section can be found and what color of ribbon attached to the hymnal to put in there. We recognize that guests often come late, so we make sure that we have several hymnals already prepared for them."

Pastor Paul Kibler at Resurrection, Cary, NC, uses the hymnbook in a traditional way that is also visitor sensitive. "We're informally formal, and we're traditionally nontraditional. Since we have visitors every Sunday, we try to gear the service toward them while following the liturgy out of the book. Basically, we lead people along. I always begin with the welcome and set the tone for the day. We let the service flow, but let the people know where we are."

Kibler uses phrases like the following: "We're on page 56." "We're going to confess our sins." "We're going to hear God's promise of forgiveness; that's what this section is all about." "Okay, folks, we're going to celebrate God's forgiveness, and we're going to sing a hymn of praise." "Now we're going to listen to the Word." "Now we're going to have the children's sermon." "Now we're going to take an offering." "We're going to give thanks for that offering, and we're going to sing an offertory."

Greeting and Effective Follow-Through

Pastor Warren Arndt shares some ideas to help visitors feel welcome in a larger church. At Faith in Troy, MI, visitor's parking is nearer the door; they ask members to walk the farther distance. He says openness to new people begins in the parking lot.

Arndt concentrates his efforts on custom planning the worship service for outreach. Each Sunday service is different. Believing it's important for people to easily enter worship life, he prints out each service.

Music plays a major part. Faith developed sets of hymn medleys—a few stanzas each for three to six songs in a row, some traditional, some Gospel, and some contemporary. The singing of praise is given a significant portion of worship time.

Arndt has "stopped identifying visitors by having them raise their hand. We used to do that. Then we would give them a welcome brochure and a packet of information. We still let them know that the packet of information is available, but we no longer make them raise their hands because many of them, we sensed, want to keep their anonymity when they come to a large church as a visitor."

Many of these churches use nametags on Sunday morning. Pastor Paul Meyer of Salem in Orange, CA, uses a unique follow-up system. "We have a card system with green cards for visitors and blue cards for members. They're in the pew. During the church service we ask people during the announcements to put their names on the appropriate cards and to tear off the lapel label and put their name on it. Then I watch for the green name tags and give those people a little extra time as they leave the church." On Monday morning, Meyer writes notes to visitors. (He hopes to have these notes done on the cover of the next Sunday's bulletin, when he gets organized.) On Wednesday, the visitors receive those notes as well as a phone call from Meyer.

"My working assumption is that if by the time of the offering they fill out the cards, that's a strong indication that they're comfortable here, they like our style, and they're saying to us, 'Come and get us.' Last year we brought in 33 new families, representing almost 100 people. So I guess the system we're using is working."

As senior pastor at Trinity in Lisle, IL, the Rev. Arthur Beyer perceives his responsibilities as writing and designing the worship service, bulletin, and other publications. Says Beyer, "I'm convinced that worship is an evangelistic instrument. In our area the Bible classes can give us a good reputation. But non-Christians or new Christians aren't immediately attracted to that. Worship is more relational. That's our first really strong contact.

"I watch every minute, design everything to be words that communicate. We're not into rock or real contemporary alternative services; we found they really don't work for us. It's better just to have a well-done, classy, precise, yet warm and friendly service that has a lot of variety."

Beyer asks worshipers to stand at the beginning of the service. Then, after everyone is standing, Beyer encourages them to introduce themselves to each other.

Beyer's church also uses a pew-card registration system. "One side is for members to indicate their attendance, and on the other there's a whole menu of information for visitors. After those cards are collected, they immediately go to the church office." Volunteer members called Friendly Visitors "pick them up and will do drop-in calls, usually within one hour from the time these people had visited the church. The next morning they'll get a letter from me. They get a follow-up telephone call from our evangelism committee and, if they're open to it, a team will ask for an appointment to visit within a couple of days."

Perspective

Church research over the past 20 years consistently shows that people who visit a church usually return if they find a relevant message and a friendly congregation. These courageous churches exemplify these two principles as they seek to provide meaningful worship that celebrates God's loving presence in Christ through Word and Sacrament and to transform themselves into friendly, visitor-sensitive congregations.

Here again are some of the principles of celebrative worship listed in chapter 1.

- These courageous churches usually offer variety in worship services. Worship is celebrative, with at least one service more contemporary or informal. Strong, Bible-centered preaching frequently dominates worship.
- Worship occurs in a friendly atmosphere. Church members consciously work to become a caring, loving congregation.
- Worship style and communication methods are receiver-oriented. Members are visitor sensitive, provide help to them, and are open and accepting of guests.

Chapter 5

The Christian Leader
as Change Agent

To the angel of the church in Laodicea write: ... I know your
deeds, that you are neither cold nor hot. I wish you were either
one or the other!

Rev. 3:14–15

Whatever else is involved in the transition to a courageous
church, the pastors in this study indisputably indicated that pastoral
leadership is crucial. Clergy must be leaders, not only theologians
and pastors. They keenly affect the mix or implementation of principles that provides for positive change. Yet most of the pastors we
surveyed said they did not receive adequate preparation in this from
seminary training. Some learned on their own—many talking in
terms of 10-year pilgrimages to learn these skills through trial and
error, through books, seminars, and graduate programs. For others,
leadership skills came almost intuitively. Others had developed the
skills in jobs with industry prior to entering the pastoral ministry.

Reviewing the data, certain aspects of pastoral leadership surface. They include focusing on mission, showing openness to creative ideas, promoting change, taking risks, gathering staff,
equipping others for ministry, and dealing with conflict. All these
played major roles in the leadership dynamic of a courageous
church.

Focusing on Mission

The courageous churches in our study enjoy a clear focus, frequently
written as a mission statement or philosophy of ministry. They understand they can't do everything well. Therefore, sensitive to community needs, they focus their energy to serve in relevant, effective

ministries—most always prompted by the leadership of the pastor.

The Rev. John Kieschnick in Houston, TX, describes himself as a person of focus and vision. Yet, "all I really had to do was help the people of Gloria Dei organize their vision with reality. I believe God sent me here just at the right time. I shared the vision with them and then trained them to move ahead to share the vision with others." As one member adds, "Before, we thought primarily of ourselves; now we think more about others and their need for Christ."

A courageous church follows that philosophy as a hallmark. The leader serves as "optometrist," helping members see with "church growth eyes."

Sometimes a core group with this world view begins a church. This happened at Shepherd of the Hills in Onalaska, WI. Says Pastor Barrie Henke, "One of the primary strengths of the founding nucleus was an emphasis upon both evangelism and education. With our focus upon the Great Commission, we went forward in the power of the Holy Spirit."

Focus means conviction about the church's ministry, direction, and identity. The Rev. Ronald Kudick, pastor of Atonement in Glendale, AZ, helps the church spotlight its strength in Lutheran doctrine, knowing "where we stand and why we're here."

Pastor Paul Kibler in Cary, NC, believes Resurrection can double in size in the coming years. He describes the church as ready and able to see its own potential. However, growth will happen only if members remain very intentional, focused, about their ministry.

That is why Pastor John Miller at Lamb of God in Humble, TX, sees communicating vision as one of his priorities. "All members have to see their tasks aimed at making disciples. We're to be building people within the congregation and drawing people to the congregation—and receiving them well. We pursue a really aggressive strategy in terms of generating prospects."

Dr. Paul Meyer of Salem in Orange, CA, recounts the story of how he helped his church to adopt a mission statement. "To my great relief and joy," says Meyer, "we adopted the right one! Our mission statement is right on. There was no direct coaxing from me, but they had been hearing it for a long time. I know the enemy; and by nature—even by Christian nature—maintenance ministry is the norm and mission ministry is abnormal."

Showing Openness to Creative Ideas

The pastors and lay leaders of these courageous congregations model openness to new ideas. Eclectically, they borrow whatever they can to improve their ministry. They constantly look for new ideas. These pastors read, listen to tapes, subscribe to magazines, and attend workshops, seminars, and learning events. They hold workshops in their churches with guest speakers to stretch their lay leaders' vision. They hire church consultants to analyze their churches, confirm their hunches, and help them sort out the trees from the forest. They welcome external input.

Rev. Elmer Thyr, pastor of Shepherd of the Hills in Rancho Cucamonga, CA, comments, "I subscribe to everything that anybody is putting out, trying to improve on what I'm doing."

The Rev. Ronald Kudick, pastor of Atonement in Glendale, AZ, says, "Our new mission leaders worked hard to get us facilities that would fill our needs. And we were quite willing to listen to the expertise of all those who could better lead and guide."

Zion in Fairbanks annually hosts the Alaska Christian Ministries Conference, which features an outside speaker to train laity to assume positions of congregational authority and responsibility.

King of Kings in Arvada, CO, hosts workshops on Saturdays and Sundays, as well as "Ongoing Ambassadors for Christ" weekends. The congregation sent a large contingency to a "Great Commission Convocation" in St. Louis. Lay people have attended church growth seminars, "Breaking the 200 Barrier" seminars, and workshops in Michigan.

In Huntsville, AL, the Rev. Richard Lessmann observes that the congregation experienced some tensions when "the old wineskin could not handle the pressure." Lessmann views courageousness "as allowing one's creativity to flourish and have some independent thought and action. In any large organization, like a denomination, we're bound up a little too much by fear. 'What will others think?' 'Will I be accepted?' 'If we start doing something different, will we be frowned upon?' 'Will this hurt us politically?' In our denomination, there is a very strong feeling of "family" and, while there's really nothing written down, there's tremendous corporate and peer pressure to conform. Maybe the courageous part comes in being willing to risk the possibility of facing some kind of rejection to get your mission done, but not with any sense of martyrdom, not with any sense of trying to be different for the sake of it."

The leaders and churches in our survey courageously learn from others, seek out resources, and have a passion for remaining on the cutting edge.

Promoting Change

As another hallmark, courageous Christian leaders not only accept change but actively promote it. And, while the changes differ from church to church and from situation to situation, one principle remains constant: change—not for the its own sake but so that the people might grow in Christ. The outward changes reflect the spiritual change in people's lives. In fact, spiritual change engenders courageous turnaround in these churches. As Pastor Mark Teike of Trinity, Davenport, IA, says, "When the spiritual maturity grew in the majority of our people, they seemed more open to being led and used by God."

The change might require a change in leaders and/or leadership style. Staff may need to increase and upgrade. Some face the need to expand facilities and, in some cases, to move locations.

At Faith in Owasso, OK, it was the lay people who promoted change. Pastor William Diekelman reports, "I'm almost 180 degrees from where I was when I came. When I came here, I really had no idea how to start a mission group. I had no goals in mind. I had no kind of vision, even one year down the road. I was taking things one day at a time. I think one of the things that helped as much as anything was the lay leadership in the congregation who have brought me around in my thinking. There were very dedicated people pushing me!"

Sometimes, the promotion for change and readiness to change turn out to be easier than expected. The Rev. Robert J. Brown and Redeemer exemplify leadership furnished and followed. Their story also contains an unusual and impressive twist.

Redeemer, founded in 1928, is located in Evansville, a southwestern Indiana city that has long been stablized in population. Redeemer had lost about 400 members during a 10-year period. The church also experienced a long vacancy, when 10 pastors declined its call.

The people were ready for change. They participated in a church growth training experience and called a pastor with counseling skills and a history of igniting church growth.

When Brown arrived at this church, average worship attendance was down to 272. Brown asked one question: " 'Do you want to grow?' They said 'yes.' I said, 'Okay; this is how we do it.' We started to make the changes immediately."

From the start, Brown emphasized the importance of Bible study. For years, about 25 participants had attended Sunday morning Bible class. Brown, who writes all his own material, began teaching. Three weeks later, 100 people came. The program continues to expand.

Soon Redeemer started an informal Sunday service that requires no Lutheran background to participate. The church lies just five miles from Kentucky, where people come from a more "Gospel mountain" tradition; so the church incorporated another hymnal celebrating that tradition. Worship committee members, who vary in age and musical ability, pick the hymns and develop new worship forms.

In four years worship attendance grew from 272 to 407. In one year, the congregation celebrated 32 adult confirmations, and 42 in another year.

Brown and Redeemer exemplify an additional component of courage. For several years, Brown suffered from a kidney disease and spent three days a week hooked up to a kidney dialysis machine. The day after he finished our first questionnaire, he had a kidney transplant—donated by one of the members. Brown now looks forward to ministering with the gift of health.

"I can't imagine what ministry would have been like with good health during these great years of growth and change," he says. "I do know that when my health failed—and continued to—I trusted God more and more with His ways of ministry.

"Perhaps if I had had health, I would have had less trust and more problems. It really was a great joy to serve during these years of transition at Redeemer."

On the other hand, sometimes change is very difficult, even for the pastor. Pastor Michael Lutz of Immanuel in Mount Clemens, MI, comments on giving up some person-to-person ministry in favor of better overall administration. "I find this is easier said than done."

His members, too, have to adjust. "Even though they feel that the pastor needs to be at all activities, they realize that he cannot. As our staff grows, the senior pastor finds himself spending more and more time in staff relations and dealing with key lay leaders within the congregation."

Taking Risks

"If there's a courage on the part of the people here, it's their willingness to do what they see the will of the Lord being for us. Are the financial resources there? That hasn't really been the primary question for these people. The question is, is it the will of the Lord or not? If it is, then we ought to do it and the Lord will provide." So Pastor Ronald Janssen describes the risk-taking members of Holy Cross in Riverdale, GA—"not so much concerned about the bottom line as they are of every line of Scripture, as it applies to them."

This church extensively ministers to relocated Southeast Asians. Holy Cross symbolizes what courageous churches risk. "The Lord does provide, and in that sense you could call these people courageous. They have been ready to really risk our future in order to work in our present."

Risks take many forms. Members often moved forward with conviction on a project, usually a building program, when finances didn't exist. Often these courageous churches added a new staff member to help meet the community's felt needs. Sometimes risk meant trying something new in an evangelism or outreach program, in community ministry projects, worship, or ways to promote Bible study. Frequently members willingly accepted criticism from other churches, area pastors, or the denomination. Interestingly, no congregation researched shows any willingness to change traditional, theological beliefs. Indeed, they work hard to foster God's Word, while showing great openness and freedom in practice and style.

These churches and their leaders try new action even if it means risking failure. They are motivated by their desire to practically touch people's lives with the Good News of Jesus Christ.

Pastor Elmer Thyr of Shepherd of the Hill in Rancho Cucamonga, CA, explains, "I'm willing to go out on a limb. I'm not afraid of doing something different, or trying new things, or getting into trouble with the congregation or whomever. I remember I tried a

Spanish service at one of our five Christmas worship times. It was a disaster. Some people said, 'I told you so.' But it was an attempt to reach a very large segment of our community—and maybe I didn't do it right."

Risk acts out faith, trusts God, and seeks his will. The late Rev. Dennis Schiefelbein in Corpus Christi, TX, identified risk as a key factor in congregational growth. "We needed to eliminate the fear of failure from the people's minds. Failure was not final. If we tried new things; and if they failed, big deal. We could always try something else. We learn to take risks, trust God, and stretch to reach that which is beyond the reach of our own power and resources."

Pastor Michael Gibson, Milpitas, CA, says Mount Olive believes risk constitutes part of ministry. "We're willing to fail for the purpose of reaching other people with the Gospel. And we do fail occasionally; but that's okay, because we really celebrate our successes. I think it's that ability to trust God for what we would seem to think was impossible, and then giving it a try that brings the successes in our ministry."

At Good Shepherd in Collinsville, IL, the Rev. Dennis Kastens sees himself as a risktaker, especially in launching Good Shepherd's school. "If there were a trap door, many times I just would have folded and looked for the first train out of town because we do such risky things. But we manage by the skin of our teeth. I'm not a Robert Schuller. It's our natural inclination to hold back and say it can't be done; it's too risky. You just have to keep telling yourself that with God all things are possible."

Immanuel, Palatine, IL, with a full range of programs and a large Christian school with 15 full-time teachers, steady growth in worship, increasing by 236 worshipers of the Lord in a five-year period, definitely takes risks; but, as Pastor Eisold observes, risk often brings failure. "You have to be willing to lick your wounds, cut your losses, and move on," he explains. "Let's say you start 30 projects a year, and 10 of them work, but 20 fail. At the end of the year you're ahead by 10. That's better than being a church that tries nothing."

Gathering Staff

Most churches will consider stretching their limits in order to enter significant debt for buildings or land, but the courageous churches in this study often did so for the sake of adding staff in anticipation of growth. They hire, for example, evangelists, administrators of spiritual gifts, directors of church growth, directors of assimilation, ministers of music, and ministers of worship, believing new staff will aid growth in quantity and quality of disciples who in turn will put their faith in action in talent, time, and treasure.

Though they did not have the finances at the time, Redeemer in Stuart, FL, added a family minister position. Pastor Dean Pingel reports it as "a leap of faith," as a necessity if they were to carry out the ministry God had given them.

Demonstrating sensitivity to the felt needs of church members and the community, the Rev. John Frerking of Faith in North Palm Beach, FL, plans to add a parish nurse. A large number of elderly people there, without family members nearby, require transportation, housing, legal counsel, day care, and medicines.

Epiphany in Chandler, AZ, has added staff in order to start a satellite church. Pastor Larry Stoterau says the congregation has called an assistant pastor to help expand the ministry at the second location and to help in Epiphany's ministry. They plan for the satellite church to become a separate mission when it is ready.

Adding staff brings changes. Pastor Glenn Brauer of Tallmadge Church in Tallmadge, OH, indicates additional staff will force change in his own ministry style—dropping out of certain areas of work—and threaten his personal comfort zone. Typical of pastoring smaller churches, Brauer remembers when he did just about everything. "We're in the position now where we need staff people. If we're going to be a creative church, I think we'll come too [that] realization."

Many of the courageous churches in our study are adding "home grown" staff from within the congregation. Staff whom God raises from within the congregation already identify and take ownership in the church's philosophy of ministry. In addition, these people work in harmony with existing staff because they've already proven they can.

For example, Good Shepherd in Gardendale, AL, is adding an evangelism director from the congregation. Pastor Richard Elseroad says, "He has an interesting past. He's proven himself, and he's really dedicated. He's a hard working person, and his resolve is just tremendous. He knows what it's like to be challenged in life, and he's really going to be helpful."

Other churches work with part-time workers raised from within the congregation. This model allows churches to grow through the "middle steps" of staffing, allowing them to staff for growth in unique area needs as their size expands until they call/contract for full-time workers.

Perhaps the church holding the record for part-time workers is Christ in Southwick, MA, served by the Rev. Jeffrey King. The congregation recently hired its 12th part-time person! Christ's fascinating ministry includes outreach to the large Jamaican population involved in migrant agricultural work as well as to area Anglos. King remarks, "We have a membership of over 500, but I would say that about 200 of those are Jamaicans. Consequently, we have these Jamaicans that are under-shepherds who live right at the migrant camp. These Jamaicans handle the ministry there to a great degree."

Faith in Troy, MI, the largest church in our study, enjoys continuous growth. In the past 7 years, the church's average Sunday attendance rose from 968 in 1983 to 1,431 in 1989. In 1991, attendance has been above 1,700 the majority of the time and over 2,000 several times. Adult confirmations are consistently 100–150 people. In addition to the Rev. Warren Arndt (Faith's pastor for the past 18 of its 25 years), the congregation now includes 2 assistant pastors, and 14 others with titles such as minister of family life, director of missions, and director of children's ministries. "From serving alone to pastoring a ministry staff of 17, it's been an exciting journey," recounts Arndt. "With each new staff (except 3) called from within the congregation, our potential for outreach grew. We developed into a staff-run church.

"This affected our style of government along the way. Voters' meetings were quickly obsolete and turned into occasional reporting sessions to the main body of the parish. The trust level of staff, council, and boards was high because the visible results were quite evident." Arndt says Faith members supported and encouraged his pastoral leadership from the beginning. He believes he and the church "teamed" well. "I really feel that this congregation has certainly given me a lot of latitude and put a lot of confidence in my leadership," he says. "Of course, you have to give and earn respect over a period of time."

Arndt works for diversified staffing. He searches for "spiritually alive" staff and elders who courageously share their love for Jesus and practice a balanced, creative ministry style. He gives special care to staff selection and feels most confident placing people who come from the congregation.

Equipping Others for Ministry

Leaders of courageous churches see themselves as equipping people for ministry rather than just ministering to people. This finds expression in both developing full or part-time staff, often from within the congregation, but also in training and developing Spirit-led volunteer lay leaders.

Gloria Dei in Houston lies in a rapidly growing suburb. The church, founded in 1966, called Pastor John Kieschnick in 1974. When he arrived, church attendance averaged about 160. In 1983 it was 504. By 1990 the average was 860.

Kieschnick raised the growth expectation of church leaders and then members. "As one member told me, 'You've turned us inside out. Before, we thought primarily of ourselves. Now we think more about others and their need for Christ.' That commitment has grown into sending 25 percent of our offering for the work of the church-at-large.

"Early on, I used an 'expanding leadership' group. I shared the vision with them and then trained them to move ahead and share the vision with others. Gloria Dei adds professional staff as quickly as feasible: first a part-time and then a full-time director of Christian education, a minister of music, a minister of youth, a minister of outreach and assimilation, and a full-time business manager. Most recently, a director of growth ministries was added to develop numerous small groups. While the church has not refilled a position of associate pastor, plans are underway to call a pastor to the newly created position of director of counseling ministries. "If we continue to add ordained staff, this in a very subtle way says to the people, 'You don't own the ministry,' " believes Kieschnick.

Because 25 percent of the members turn over each year, the church has emphasized small groups in the past six years as a way to bring people into relationships. In addition to these, each elder serves 160 members in "a small congregation." Kieschnick points out that each elder now serves as many people as he did when he began pastoral ministry there. Kieschnick says key church leaders were ready to move forward. "The Holy Spirit had made the congregation and community ripe for growth. So, all I really had to do was help them organize their vision with reality. What we're trying to say in a very bold way is, 'Folks, you do own the ministry.' We really want to emphasize the priesthood of all believers."

Redeemer in Stuart, FL, attributes their activation of laity to the Rev. Donn Abdon's Parish Leadership seminars. "The church was changed five years ago when we restructured under the Abdon program. The lay leadership has taken a very active role in the life of this parish," says Pastor Dean Pingel. "The pastoral staff has been much more involved in counseling and doesn't have near enough time to be in contact with the members on a one-to-one basis." By activating members into ministry, the parish has continued to grow rapidly.

The Rev. Stephen Wagner in Carrollton, TX, sees involving and equipping the people as essential to the church, particularly for multiplying small-group ministries. "Now we don't even start groups unless there's leadership identified for a new group. And they've added a new component; a person's leadership for a new group is validated when he or she finds an assistant who will eventually take over the group. The highest value we place on the groups is that they will reproduce themselves."

Such an equipping ministry requires trust—trust that lay people will do ministry, and trust that God works through His people to minister the Gospel in this world. A powerful expression of this takes place when lay people lead the entire worship service in the pastor's absence. "When I'm gone, my elders preach," says the Rev. Henry Biar of King of Kings in San Antonio, TX. "They have the whole service. For example, one will lead the liturgy, one will do the readings, and one will preach."

Another aspect of equipping ministry means people aren't elected for the short-term but, in a stronger biblical approach, are "called" to ministry. Trinity, Walden, NY, exemplifies this. Pastor Raymond Cummings says, "As people experienced new life with Jesus and new people were coming into the church who had deep personal needs and questions, it became evident that the kind of eldership that was functioning was ineffective. It became clear that elders would have to be trained who could work with the pastor in shepherding the flock. Therefore we elected individuals who had a personal love for the Bible and a love and desire to minister to people and to work with a pastor."

Pastor Cummings describes the nature of this call. "Elders were asked to make a lifetime commitment to their office. They could be voted out by the congregation if there was a problem, but they were to see their calling and development as a call from God to work within the congregation as servants. Elders then became involved with the pastor in his work, praying, visiting the sick, working with problems, counseling, leading home cell groups, and seeking God for the ongoing vision of the congregation."

Another powerful expression of trust in God's people to plan and implement their ministry is at Grace, in De Witt, IA. Pastor Ronald Goodsman explains, "I just throw out ideas. I always tell the congregation, 'If you don't like this idea, I'm capable of more than one good idea.' They think there'll be another one coming. Some ministers take an idea and think their ministry is either going to stand or fall on it. Well, I don't anymore. I just keep shooting ideas at these people for whichever ones they take." One of those was the calling of a director of Christian education. Another idea that worked was to begin a daughter church in nearby Maquoketa in 1987. Goodsman considers his job as being pastor—not trustee, elder, president, or treasurer. He doesn't attend any nominating committee or make suggestions. When the committee meeting reaches the point of putting together the budget, he announces he's going to the Tastee Freez—and leaves. "The essence of leadership is that once the congregation has decided a matter, and I've spoken neither for or against, I can encourage them all to follow," he explains.

Sometimes, pastors come to a congregation where lay leaders are already energized. The Rev. Thomas Teske in Arvada, CO, says a "new beginning" occurred in King of Kings before his arrival. During the pastoral vacancy lay leaders realized the church must change if it was to witness effectively to its community. Members changed from a survival to a growth mode. "In the next couple of years there was a definite change in focus, leading to a strong desire to reach out with the Gospel to those who did not know Christ," says Teske. Their vision grew more solid after some church leaders attended a church-growth workshop. The third step happened when the church adopted a mission statement, 'Making Disciples Who Love and Serve.'

Dealing with Conflict

With growth comes change; and with change comes conflict. In just about every courageous church studied, significant conflict exists or existed.

The pastors and key leaders of these churches deal with conflict positively. First, they accept that it comes with the territory, and are not surprised by its presence. No leader likes it, but they understand it as a natural consequence of acting courageously. Second, they confront it when necessary and ignore it when helpful. But whatever action they take, they take intentionally. Third, the leaders do not let the conflict program their ministries. While they are sensitive and open to people who disagree with them or the church's direction, they do not let noisy and negative detractors consume their energy or set their agendas. Finally, the leaders accept the fact that they can not please everyone. They realize that some people will need help in finding another church that better meets their needs.

Interestingly, internal conflict sometimes precipitates change rather than results from change. As Pastor Doepel of Cross of Christ in Chattanooga, TN, reports, "The church went through a difficult time with the previous pastor. It wasn't his fault—he had a health problem. But this hampered his performance, and it really made the congregation ready to do something."

At Resurrection in Cary, NC, the church had suffered a split due to internal conflict over the nature of Christian life. When Pastor Paul Kibler came on the scene, people wanted reconciliation and peace in Christ and with each other. The conflict prepared the way for openness among the remaining members and provided a healthy setting for new members. God used that healing for rapid growth.

More commonly, congregations experience conflict because of the changes and challenges that growth brings. This happens especially as churches move through the "200 barrier" and long-term members comprehend that the family atmosphere is changing. Pastor Paul Moldenhauer of First in Charlotte, MI, talks about their struggles. "Some real precious and strong leaders of the church in those earlier days didn't like the direction the church was going. I think it was largely based on a feeling of loss of control. There was a sense that it was not going to be the same, small family that it always was. They either had to learn to live with it or . . . in several cases, they just got fed up and left. This was a real burden to me . . . a real burden to me."

Sometimes conflict occurs because of a change in worship services. Pastor Richard Mayer of St. John in Lawton, OK, says adding a second service became a very complicated obstacle for St. John. Of all the goals accomplished at St. John, he believes this met with the greatest resistance.

Pastor Ronald Zehnder of St. Luke in Ann Arbor, MI, who refers to himself as "mildly charismatic," responded to dramatic increases in worship attendance by developing four weekend worship services. "Two of them are traditional, the third contemporary, and the newest is a more open praise service. All are eucharistic and always include confession, absolution, and a structured liturgy. However," he says, "I remember one pastor's wife, a widow, who came to our contemporary service. I had a children's message, and there probably were a few jokes in the sermon. On the way out of church she said, 'Is this a Missouri Synod church?' I said 'Yes.' And she responded, 'Well, I never!' and just walked off. I knew we'd never see her again."

When dealing with conflict, the Rev. Dennis Kastens uses the word "persevering." As pastor of Good Shepherd at Collinsville, IL, Kastens notes that it means "just a lot of diligence and not letting up. It means just keep doing what you're doing."

Leaders of courageous churches suffer pain because of criticism and jealousy. As Pastor J. Arthur Cox of Grace in Bradford, PA, says, "It hurt when I discovered that someone [in our own congregation] had misinterpreted what we were doing. They were saying that we were just trying to build a big church so that Art Cox can get some glory. I understand that. It goes on in any church that's growing. But it still hurts when you hear it. It doesn't come from the key leaders, though. They know better. It comes from those who are on the fringes of activity within the congregation."

Some distrust comes from outside the congregation. Pastor Barrie Henke of Shepherd of the Hill in Onalaska, WI, explains, "There have been times when we pretty much stood alone. And there was a lot of distrust because we were growing. Some said that we must be growing because we were doing something wrong or something contrary. It gets uncomfortable when you deal with this distrust among your [pastoral] brethren. Sometimes you meet with the brothers so that you can get strengthened, but often it doesn't happen."

God gives strength and help to deal with and overcome the hurt caused by conflicts and differences. Pastor Warren Arndt of Faith in Troy, MI, wishes people would follow the Lord's teaching in Matthew 18 to go directly to a person causing problems. "What offends me the most in the church today is that if somebody has a disagreement with you—and sometimes clergy seem to be the worst—they gossip. How sad, when the people who start these rumors never pick up the phone and call you, or they never come over and say, 'Hey, listen, I don't understand what you're doing here,' or challenge you, or write you a letter or anything like that. I feel sorry, because those individuals seldom ask the right questions of the right people."

Pastor Jeffrey King of Christ in Southwick, MA, fights hurt with a sense of humor. "One church in our community even sent out a letter to all its members to beware of me personally, saying I was preaching a foreign gospel, a gospel that was all positive thinking, fun and games . . . One pastor called what I was doing 'McWorship,' like McDonalds. I thought about it and came to the conclusion that that was really a great compliment. Who attracts more people than McDonalds? If we can present Christ and our confessional beliefs in a way that would attract as many people as McDonalds, that would be tremendous!"

Perspective

Leadership studies in American culture repeatedly recognize the importance of two different philosophies and behaviors: One is care-oriented to people, the other is activity-oriented to tasks.

People-oriented leadership behavior recognizes how followers feel about themselves and the situation, affirms and gives individual attention, assures fair treatment, and builds relationships between people. Task-oriented leadership behavior focuses on accomplishing goals, offers organizing techniques to fulfill them, and gives assistance when necessary.

While the leaders in our study use both in their leadership, they usually show that mission activity takes precedence over supportive relationships at some time. These leaders display task-oriented behaviors because mission itself is goal-directed. It reaches out with Christ to the unchurched. And the growth in these churches gives evidence that task-oriented behaviors are working and effective.

This has not eliminated support-oriented behavior by these leaders. They give great attention to relationships between church members and their personal relationships with each other—conditioned, however, by their activity orientation for mission.

A test of leadership styles comes when opposition to the mission arises. In almost every case in this study, a few and sometimes many members became unhappy with their church's new direction. Believing that support-orientation tends to set aside the trouble-causing goal so that peace can be restored and, thereby, allow growth to level off, these task/mission-oriented ministers keep pulling—even in the face of opposition. The external mission of outreach seems more important than some unhappy members.

Of course, the best leadership combines both orientations. Leaders can accomplish both. Pastor Elmer Thyr, Shepherd of the Hill, Rancho Cucamonga, CA, clearly makes mission as his own first priority, keeping all eyes focused on it lest the young church become too comfortable with itself along the way. But, recognizing his personal limitations in supporting individuals once they come into fellowship, he looks to other staff who can.

Pastor Warren Arndt, Faith, Troy, MI, also effectively builds a staff able to develop and maintain supportive relationships—and do so with many more people than he could individually.

On the other hand, Pastor Ronald Goodsman, Grace, De Witt, IA, thinks of himself as highly support-oriented. But he too sets tasks—building a church camp and a home for the elderly—to extend mission in this tradition-oriented church. He is continually "shooting ideas at these people for whichever ones they take." He doesn't emphasize growth as his main goal, but it happens by pursuing missions beyond the norm.

After reflection, the Rev. Ingo Dutzmann (Redeemer, Cape Elizabeth, ME) knows he came on too forcefully with Redeemer's people in setting activity-oriented tasks and undoubtedly will be more temperate if called to a new church.

In summary, while the shepherd image continues to be a viable and favorite model among pastors and church leaders, and is strongly fostered in theological education because of the biblical imagery, it inherently is oriented to preservation of the flock by the shepherd. In most of the cases we studied, leadership holds out a mission vision and brings about appropriate changes to accomplish mission tasks. Strong pastoral leadership, especially in larger churches, consciously limits personal shepherding to staff and key leaders and their families and places more time on visioning, communicating, coordinating relationships, and the overall mission of the congregation. The sheep are expected to care for and to produce more sheep.

Let's review again some of the principles discussed in chapter 1:

- The lay as well as professional leaders in a courageous church are people of vision. Understanding both broad objectives and specific goals, they present clear direction.

- The Christian leaders work for change, and the congregations accept change. The leaders understand possible barriers to change and growth, and the churches are flexible in meeting the challenge barriers present.

- Risk is acceptable and people have permission to fail. In faith in God's promises, the professional and lay leaders try things that seem humanly impossible. The congregations attempt action never taken before.

- The churches provide staff in anticipation of growth rather than responding to growth that has taken place. Leadership is active, rather than reactive. Often, staff is "home grown" as leaders find people within the congregation and groom them for professional staff positions, into which they are certified.

- The leaders manage conflict, accepting it as a necessary part of change in a growing congregation. Leaders know how to minister to negative, subjective, nongrowth people who often show their teeth at meetings. These pastors and lay leaders don't allow the "alligators" to set the agenda, though they recognize that some people will disagree with the congregation's direction.

- The pastor and key leaders possess perseverance.

- In these congregations, the (senior) pastor considers himself to be, and the church views him as, the congregational leader.
- The professional leaders equip the laity. They see their primary job as motivating, releasing, and training laity through a preaching and teaching ministry. These leaders strongly emphasize the priesthood of all believers.
- The professional leaders deal intentionally with people who develop hurt feelings or other negative responses to the growing church. They accept that reaction (and their feelings about it) as part of what happens when serving a church in a courageous manner.
- The professional leaders strongly attempt to remain on the cutting edge of ministry through continuing education. They constantly look for new ideas, attend seminars, read books, listen to tapes, and often engage in postgraduate work. They also motivate key congregational leaders to do likewise.

Chapter 6

A People-Centered Ministry

"My food," said Jesus, "is to do the will of Him who sent me and to finish His work. Do you not say, 'Four months more and then the harvest'? I tell you, open your eyes and look at the fields! They are ripe for harvest. Even now the reaper draws his wages, even now he harvests the crop for eternal life, so that the sower and the reaper may be glad together. Thus the saying 'One sows and another reaps' is true. I sent you to reap what you have not worked for. Others have done the hard work, and you have reaped the benefits of their labor."

Many of the Samaritans from that town believed in him because of the woman's testimony, "He told me everything I ever did." So when the Samaritans came to Him, they urged Him to stay with them, and He stayed two days. And because of His words many more became believers.

They said to the woman, "We no longer believe just because of what you said; now we have heard for ourselves, and we know that this man really is the Savior of the world."

John 4:34–42

While the churches in our study are goal-oriented toward an *end*—making disciples (see ch. 2)—they are strongly relationship-oriented in their *means*—dealing with people. Therefore, these churches constantly look for opportunities to touch people with the Gospel "where they are" in life. It's a very person-to-person style of servanthood.

In part, this means reaching out with a "felt needs" ministry that provides a bridge over which the love of Christ flows and the good news of the Gospel advances.

These ministry-minded churches show themselves as positive ministries of Law and Gospel. They edify individuals by being high on encouragement and low on criticism. Because the members are excited about their Lord and their ministries, an inviting enthusiasm marks their corporate cultures.

Centered on people, these churches deliberately work to understand the context, the community, in which the people live—and plan ministry accordingly. They make ministry indigenous, fitting the context, whether urbanites, Mexican Americans, Laotians, Jamaican migrant workers, new Floridians basking in the sunlight of retirement, baby boomers, yuppies, or upwardly mobile blacks. These churches recognize the uniquenesses of singles, youth, families, high-tech engineers, suburbanites, and unchurched traditional Christians. Whatever the group, these churches develop evangelism strategies for each. Though single-minded and unswerving in purpose, they demonstrate innovation and flexibility in style and strategy.

These courageous churches manifest mission-mindedness even as they incorporate, or include new members. They sincerely work to make disciples, not add names to an institutional roll. They aspire to assimilate people and make them feel included. They "fold" people into the body of Christ. These ministry-minded churches promote the New Testament "glue" of fellowship and work to create a family atmosphere in which relationship-building is important.

Meeting Felt Needs

Courageous congregations analyze their communities, discover felt needs among the people, and develop innovative strategies to serve those needs as a vehicle for the Gospel.

Consider, for example, King of Kings in Chesterfield, MO. Recognizing that mothers of preschool children need free time to shop, relax, or enjoy a leisurely lunch, the church provides a ministry to children (and mothers) called "Mother's Day Out." Pastor Bachert senses a need for people to get together in small groups and share their Christian life together. To help him meet the need, he earned his doctor of ministry with an emphasis in starting small-group fellowships—people meeting in the houses of members for prayer, Bible study, and fellowship.

Trinity in Lisle, IL, began a preschool and day-care center, attracting single parents. Next they sought a grant to develop Helpmates, a ministry to divorced Christians—a ministry which now has 17 chapters in various congregations.

For Pastor John Frerking of Faith in North Palm Beach, FL, "The latch-key situation was something the community called a crisis. We saw it as an opportunity. We began to gear our whole church to really think about children not as a problem but as a potential. And we began to make the necessary changes to implement a program. It required a lot of commitment, faith, and hope. It required us to build another building and put staff together to handle the enormous number of kids. Today we have 250 children in our after-school program. The children aren't only watched and kept safe and secure, but we're actually able to perform ministry for Christ within this setting through teaching, telling Bible stories, and helping them understand the Christian way of life."

Pastor Michael Gibson in Milpitas, CA, realized many un-churched, hurting people lived in his community. He wrote a sermon series called "Where Is God When You Hurt?" Weekly, he encouraged members to think and pray about people they knew who were hurting—and to invite and bring friends to the worship service for a particular topic. "It was really exciting," reports Gibson. "It seems like they could all identify people and say, 'I know you're hurting; why don't you come? Our pastor's going to talk on God helping us in times of hurt.' "

Our Savior in Centereach, NY, began a preschool in its Long Island community. "We serve the neighborhood," says Pastor Ronald Stelzer. "Every year we draw a few people who become members through the program. The preschool children occasionally sing in church. That gives us an excuse to expose the parents to our Sunday morning worship which otherwise might not happen."

At Family of Christ in Andover, MN, Pastor Thomas Braun says, "Perhaps some might think we go a little overboard trying to meet the needs of people, but I think it really pays off. There are a lot of people who come in looking for spiritual guidance. They're new to the community, or they've had hurt feelings from another church. This is a church where someone will listen to their needs and their feelings. We tell them if they're going to get serious about their problems, they need to be in the Word of God and experience His love. I would say a good percentage, at least 30–35 percent of our growth, comes each year from hurting people, some from other churches. We have a lot of ministry for recovering alcoholics and dysfunctional families."

Resurrection in Cary, NC, serves as a center for a Meals on Wheels program. Members also initiated a pan-Lutheran group that developed a house for the homeless.

Good Shepherd, Collinsville, IL, meets felt needs through an extensive co-ed athletic program conducted on their 14-acre athletic field. They require that some unchurched prospects be on every team.

Pastor Jeffrey King of Southwick, MA, "discovered that busy people and people with a low commitment level fear getting 'roped into' a long, ongoing Bible study. So we began to offer an 'Adult Personal Growth Program' based on a catalog of special short-term seminars (from one to six one-hour sessions). These seminars are need-centered. Twice a year, we provide 'miniseminars' held during the worship service on topics I feel are extremely important, such as spiritual gifts and "Heart to Heart" evangelism. On these Sundays, the liturgy is shortened, and half the worship hour is a classroom-style presentation complete with handouts and study sheets. This enables us to reach our entire active membership rather than the committed minority that will attend a special class."

Meeting felt needs affects worship, too. Pastor Glenn Brauer says, "Tallmadge is a very young congregation. Many of the people who come here are new and younger people. They want to sing some 'up-tempo' music. They want to sing some things that are more Gospel-oriented and still have proper theological principles in them. So we've made some changes. Our worship attendance has picked up since that time."

Being sensitive to felt needs also leads to church planting. Pastor John Miller of Humble, TX, says some members had a 30-minute drive from Kingwood, and many prospects were not coming to Lamb of God services. So the church met their need for accessible worship by starting a congregation there.

These examples and many others show creative approaches to meeting felt needs.

Showing a Positive Spirit

A spirit of positive optimism characterizes the courageous churches in our study. When God ignites the environment and potential for change and growth, the pastor and lay leaders feel it—and their enthusiasm adds to the mix creating a courageous church.

Pastor William Diekelman of Faith in Owasso, OK, says one factor contributing to Faith's growth is that the congregation is positive, enthusiastic, and "has no fear of failure."

In Bakersfield, CA, Pastor Theodore Hartman of St. John believes "our congregation has a greater confidence in the power of the Lord because He got us through the changes. That's like the trial by fire that leaves the victor exhausted but secure. I think our congregation is even more open to the Lord's leading," a point that illustrates what church growth people call a "growth mode."

When Emmaus in Milwaukee, WI, made the transition from a primarily white congregation to a congregation reaching a black community, people encouraged each other during the transition and felt strong expectancy and hope for the future. Pastor Ahlborn says, "Our people have matured greatly. They actively encourage and spur one another on. Can you imagine a church where black and white work together, pray together, celebrate together, and share grief together? We have it. We know that whites in the foreseeable future will be the minority at Emmaus; yet there's no evidence of resentment. Rather there's joy that we're reaching people."

Pastor Raymond Cummings at Trinity in Walden, NY, is excited about the future, even after being there 20 years. "The church has gradually grown into an exciting place. It has a positive, upbeat kind of atmosphere and we really have a sense of calling and ministry. It feels like I'm starting over again."

Pastor Jon Reusch of Hope in Warren, MI, remembers how the people's excitement captured his attention in his first visit. He explains, "We met the people, and there was a core group of very friendly people. They were very committed. They were eager to have someone come into this church and turn things around."

Pastor Paul Moldenhauer in Charlotte, MI, speaks of First Church's expectant mood: "There's an enthusiasm, optimism and excitement over what God has done and will do at First and in the members' lives. We have a new attitude. It's an attitude of enthusiasm about what Christ has done for us, that He is alive, and that He makes a difference in our everyday lives."

Pastor Richard Elseroad of Good Shepherd in Gardendale, AL, says, "I think we're in a very good position. That's why I think we're going to grow. I'm confident about that, and I'm enthusiastic." Probably, most of Good Shepherd's people have caught Elseroad's confidence and enthusiasm, and believe in the vision for what God can and will do.

Courageous congregations and their pastors express and live out a positive spirit. Visitors catch that enthusiasm and sense that something exciting is happening among the people of God—which attracts more people to the church, which fuels more excitement. A God-given growth momentum!

Doing Ministry in Its Context

A courageous church fits its context, or setting. Pastor Warren Arndt of Troy, MI, explains. "I think a courageous church is a church that understands its own authenticity and the culture in which the church resides. It's a church that's willing to create programs, ministries, styles, and functions that relate in a relevant way to that culture. It's a church that's also able to stay sound to the teaching of the church and represent its doctrines properly. Yet it's bold enough to change the style to meet the context."

Pastor Ronald Stelzer of Centereach, NY, describes Our Savior's context. "The Catholic Church is largely represented in our area," he continues. "I think a lot of Catholics get disgusted or confused, then they look for an alternative. I think we, as a Lutheran church, do have enough similarities to draw some of those people who don't want to totally reject their background. Consequently, Our Savior takes care to be sensitive to Roman Catholics who are seeking a new church fellowship."

Trinity in Walden, NY, responds to a socioeconomically depressed area. Pastor Raymond Cummings says, "We opened a storefront ministry in our community because we see a need to reach out with concern to the poor. There's a high percentage of welfare and disadvantaged people in our area."

St. John, an old downtown church founded in 1916 in Lawton, OK, "changed locations" without moving. Lawton, the third-largest city in Oklahoma, had been declining for some time, and the future looked bleak. But in the late 1970s, the city bulldozed 10 blocks and developed a large shopping mall in the center of town. People from around the area regularly travel to shop within two blocks of the church. So St. John holds confirmation and membership classes on Sunday afternoon to fit in with people's shopping schedules. In 1983 Sunday attendance had averaged 119; by 1989 it had grown to 275 and the church dedicated an 11,000-square-foot fellowship hall and classroom addition to the existing 7,000 square-feet. The Rev. Richard Mayer considers a more informal church service format and Law/Gospel sermons with visual aids significant factors in the church's growth.

King of Kings, San Antonio, TX, grudgingly began in 1975 with a small group of 50 older people when their previous congregation left the denomination—and abandoned the property, with its significant debt, to these small few. Although they believed that they could continue, with district help, to reach out through their neighborhood-context church, the district convinced them (against their will, it turned out) to sell the property and begin a new congregation in an entirely new context some 14 miles away in a fast-growing area of San Antonio, and to call a new pastor.

The Rev. Henry Biar arrived with enthusiasm and a vision of growth and community service within the new community. The 50 founding members did not. Finally, after the departure of some of the original 50 who were hurt, angry, and discouraged, and after the reception of new members from the new community, King of Kings was able to establish itself in the new context. As one example of the conflict in contextualizing itself, King of Kings established a day-care center. When one of the original couples threatened to leave (with their large contributions) if the center were not closed, pastor Biar said, "Well, I'm sorry to see you go. But this is part of our ministry. People come here, and they see that we care about their children [and] say, 'If you care about that, how about our spiritual welfare?' "

Interestingly, the congregation again needs change according to its context: a Mexican-American population in the area. As part of that outreach, the church offers a Spanish Bible study led by Mexican-American members whom the church is helping to learn biblical teaching through the use of a Spanish catechism. Biar said, "I can't speak Spanish, so I gave the leader a Spanish catechism, which helps him speak to them a lot easier."

Prince of Peace, Carrollton, TX, also has a ministry to Hispanic people—in their location, teaching them English.

The context for the Rev. Larry Stoterau of Epiphany, Chandler, AZ, is twofold: a suburban community southeast of Phoenix, growing primarily with young families, and Sun Lakes, a growing retirement area eight miles to the south, which forms the nucleus of their satellite church.

St. John, in Bakersfield, CA, a growing city in the San Joaquin Valley, is now serving in two contexts. The original church, founded in 1910, was for most of its history an established, downtown congregation of modest size. In 1975, it relocated to the rapidly growing southwestern part of Bakersfield—a new context for ministry, but still its only one. They also began a school, despite failure with a school at their old location. Integration of long-time and new members of various Christian backgrounds caused tension, but the church brought together the best of the traditional and the new.

At that time, the church committed itself to staffing in anticipation of growth in its new context. Besides the Rev. Theodore Hartman, who came in 1985, as senior pastor, program staff includes an associate pastor, directors of youth and children's ministry, and ministers of church growth and music.

Recently, however, St. John leaders saw ahead a major transition in context. They want to develop a satellite congregation on a 10-acre location five miles away, where population growth is booming. Besides conducting a church service, they expect to move their day school and recreational programs there. The special challenge they face is to view themselves as members of the same congregation while participating in different ministries at two locations.

For Good Shepherd, Collinsville, IL, the context is not so much the local as it is its socioeconomic group: baby boomers. The average age of the membership is 34. Good Shepherd recognizes that this group wants choices, and it operates with a megachurch mind-set. And although living in a slow-growth and highly churched area just 11 miles east of downtown St. Louis, Good Shepherd continues to follow a path of steady growth of 5 to 10 percent a year. The average attendance of 279 in 1978 (the year before the Rev. Dennis Kastens' arrival) grew to 616 in 1989. About 95 percent of the members commune regularly. Although it hasn't happened yet, the congregation envisions itself becoming a megachurch.

For Holy Cross in Riverdale, GA, contextual ministry means reaching Laotians with a full-time Laotian lay minister.

In Southwick, MA, for his ministry to Jamaicans held in the mess hall of the migrant workers' camp, Pastor Jeffrey King recruits help among Jamaican leaders. At the service, King only preaches the sermon and teaches adult instruction. "Jamaican leaders lead the songs," he says. "They know how to lead those songs where the people stand and clap their hands and sing the folk Gospel choruses. They like a lot of emotion in their worship, and they like it loud."

The late Rev. Dennis Schiefelbein at Corpus Christi, TX, said that Mexican-Americans there love to "party and barbecue. Therefore, we have many parties and barbecues that celebrate accomplishments, and we announce what's being recognized and celebrated."

While it seems obvious to include a Laotian for work among the Laotians in Georgia and a Jamaican for work among the migrant Jamaican workers in Massachusetts, it points to a basic definition important to reaching out with the Gospel to people in their context: People gather in "people groups," segments of society whose members feel an affinity toward each other and identify with each other. Identifying people groups has helped the churches in this study to develop specific evangelism strategies.

Consider again the people groups served by the churches mentioned in the previous paragraphs—in addition to the Laotians and Jamaicans, people with a Catholic background; the socioeconomically depressed; downtown shoppers; new suburbanites; Hispanics; and baby boomers. Contrary to the common view that only race determines people groups, in reality homogeneous groups can be identified by lifestyle, culture, worldview, or economic status, as well as by ethnicity.

Pastor Marvin Ahlborn notes the change in people groups at Emmaus in Milwaukee, WI. Emmaus, founded in 1890 and with a grand history, watched its neighborhood deteriorate into the poorest part of Milwaukee's inner city. As with so many inner-city churches, Emmaus' course changed dramatically when its members, traditional German Lutherans, moved to the suburbs. About 30 years ago, Emmaus ranked as one of the largest churches in the Synod; 25 years later it had lost 2,800 members.

The neighborhood changed from white to black in the 1960s. Although the church owned several blocks in another area to which they could have moved, it chose to stay and to serve its neighborhood. It closed the floodgates, paid its bills, and met some old and created some new commitments. Currently, about 65 percent of Emmaus' 600 members are of black heritage. The two people groups are further differentiated by the white members tending to be more than 60 years old and blacks below 45 years old. More than half the students in their grade school of 100 are nonmembers, and most are black.

The Rev. Marvin Ahlborn, pastor since 1984, credits a key role in Emmaus' commitment to serve the neighborhood to the deceased pastor emeritus, Victor Selle, who at one time had been the head pastor—as was his father before him, beginning in 1920. In many respects, Milwaukee had gone through the same social upheavals usually associated with Detroit and Watts, and Emmaus too experienced its share of dissension and uncertainty. Ahlborn stresses that when factors are uncontrollable, you must adapt and serve rather than give up. Congregational members had to learn the difference between "German" and "Lutheran."

"Even though the hard times of vandalism, break-ins and downward spiral hurt many, we feel God has been good to us, and good times are here now and still ahead," he says. "Because with our various ministries we have earned the right to be here, our problems have greatly fallen off. The community accepts and cares for us."

Although the church continues to confront frustrating financial limitations, many member "alumni" assist. Emmaus, "mother" to other churches, also receives their help. Recently, the church needed $80,000 for a renovation project in the sanctuary. With additional external contributions, the congregation paid off the loan in a year-and-a-half.

The most joyful experience for Ahlborn and most members was reaching stability. "The Lord blesses us," he says. "It's a feeling that you're accomplishing something. You're serving where you're needed."

At Shepherd of the Hills in Rancho Cucamonga, CA, Pastor Elmer Thyr notes that this multiracial congregation serves a people group "based upon the upper-middle class community, and anybody who can afford to live here feels welcome and considers themselves part of the same group." Pastor Bradley Hoefs in Omaha, NE, shares his vision. "As we move toward the year 2000, large churches that can offer multiple offerings are going to be the churches that grow and are effective for the Lord. Some baby boomers will go to small churches with a lot of potential. If you look at grocery stores today, they're not just little grocery stores—they have all the things you need. That's the mind-set we're living in."

Hoefs and King of Kings are gearing to become a megachurch to include the baby-boomer people group who want the choices megachurches offer.

In summary, contextual ministry, by its very nature, works everywhere; it fits the place where God has called a particular congregation to do ministry.

Working toward Assimilation

Once any group of people know Christ and come into the church, they must be assimilated. If not folded into the church membership, many walk right out the back door. The churches in this study show great sensitivity and zeal about assimilation, and they demonstrate creativity in developing special ministries.

Grace in Huntsville, AL, created a board of assimilation. This board begins incorporating people even before they become members (as well as during their first year of membership). Pastor Richard Lessmann says this has cut down on back-door losses.

At Mount Olive in Milpitas, CA, Pastor Michael Gibson uses the adult information class as a major area for assimilation.

At Redeemer in Cape Elizabeth, ME, Pastor Ingo Dutzmann personally oversees members' assimilation. He offers them "some vital way" of involvement "beyond church and Bible study. I find out what they're good at and let them go."

Pastor Roland Kauth, Zion, Fairbanks, AK, uses a "shepherding program," with members in different geographical areas serving as shepherds and undershepherds. Kauth assigns individuals to these leaders, who maintain regular contact with "their" members, encourage them to stay involved in their cell groups (area Bible studies), and who plan social events and fellowship activities in their area.

Many courageous churches use spiritual gifts analysis to ensure assimilation. At Tallmadge Church in Tallmadge, OH, the board of elders works to match people's gifts to a ministry within six months.

First Church, Charlotte, MI, added a part-time assimilation coordinator and created a hospitality committee. This group visits new members within six months to establish friendships and to pass on church materials and information.

Cross of Christ in Chattanooga, TN, keeps individualizing uppermost and encourages constructive communication. About a dozen elders personalize care and assimilation by leading care groups. Each oversees 14–18 families and tries to keep up monthly contact. The congregation added a director of discipleship in 1988, a full-time staff person who recruits and trains members to help in assimilating new members into the congregation's ministries. An administrative assistant came on a year later. These two concentrate on inreach while Pastor Edwin Doepel works on what he loves most: outreach.

Pastor John Miller at Lamb of God in Humble, TX, hired an administrative assistant who tracks new members as they come into the church and makes sure they get involved in a task or a group within six months. New members also attend a six-session orientation experience, including a two-hour spiritual gifts seminar and a three-hour seminar on web evangelism.

Prince of Peace in Carrollton, TX, offers an extensive "Inclusion Program" for new participants. The Rev. Stephen Wagner explains, "If a person comes through the system that we've designed, and most do, they would be worshiping and communing on a regular basis; they would be in a Bible class or Sunday school; they would be in a small group; they would have communicated information to us about their spiritual gifts and personality; and they would be in the process of being recruited into a service based on what they've shared about themselves. They would also have completed a commitment card in setting goals for days of worship, days of attendance in corporate worship and Bible class, percentages of giving over a three-year period, and also specifically identified people they will be inviting." As a result of the process, the church usually has monthly contact with about 85 percent of its members, 1,100 out of 1,300.

Assimilation, of course, means more than involving individuals in the church's programs. It means meeting people's personal needs for fellowship—which includes providing the kind of Christian fellowship that enables new members to feel a part of the congregation's people group.

At Bethel, Fort Smith, AR, fellowship groups provide an important infrastructure that leads toward Bible study. Pastor Tieman says, "The internal growth we've experienced has, to a large degree, simply been a continuation of the process begun several years ago. That process included personal caring and genuine friendships developed among members themselves, using the fellowship opportunities made available by the church. Bethel is known as the place where people like to eat. Potlucks, dinners, parties, and coffee pots abound! The people have grown close participating in these fellowship activities. There's a definite correlation between the internal growth of the congregation and the number of people regularly studying the Word. We believe it's no coincidence that Bible study attendance and the use of personal devotion materials has gone up dramatically in the past couple years."

On the other hand, it's often the strong Bible study that leads to the fellowship. Rev. Rodney Otto explains how this works at St. Mark, Kentwood, MI. "The primary fellowship group in the church when I arrived eight years ago was the golf league and its parties. This has been transformed into house groups, church fellowships that revolve around the mission of the church and welcomes new members."

Pastor J. Arthur Cox at Grace in Bradford, PA, led his people to develop caring and sharing groups that study the Bible and that fellowship together. Cox says fellowship acts as the glue holding growth together.

Many courageous churches intentionally plan a fellowship program. Churches like St. Luke, Ann Arbor, MI, specifically constructed a building to produce a site for more fellowship opportunities.

Others, such as St. John, Lawton, OK, provide creative opportunities for fellowship—a gigantic January "birthday" party, a large Valentine's party, etc.

As observers of what's happening in the churches in this study, we the authors wonder if, in the future, fellowship groups might develop as small congregations within the congregation, meeting regularly (probably weekly), and offering opportunities for fellowship and Bible study during the Sunday school hour. If so, we see that as enormously assisting the ability of churches to grow larger, even into megachurches.

Whether or not that happens, these people-centered congregations have already shown that they care about building mature disciples for their Lord, for His glory.

Perspective

The churches in our study reveal five transition or change points that all congregations can face: *life-cycle* change as the church changes in size either larger or smaller, *celebrative* change as the church commemorates a significant event in its history, or in its community life, or significant events of members, *ministerial* change as a vacancy occurs in the pastoral office or its auxiliary offices, *internal* change as the church experiences challenges to the health of the network of relationships or reorganization of its forms or functions, or *external* change as the church responds to the national or local contextual or institutional threats to its existence.

The cluster of six principles culled from our research of growing churches and presented in this report can be helpful guides during all transition and change points and will help you cope with change as you seek Jesus' direction for your church. The principles of a people-centered ministry need special application at these times.

To repeat some of the principles discussed in chapter 1:

- These churches operate to meet their community's felt needs. Each church constantly investigates needs and finds vehicles to touch people's lives in relevant ways.

- The churches display a positive spirit, usually reflected by the pastor's tone and style. Members feel strong enthusiasm and a sense of renewal. An edifying atmosphere builds people up and encourages them in their faith and Christian life.

- These churches encourage fellowship and maintain a family atmosphere.

- The ministry of these churches is relevant, contextual, and indigenous. The community, not tradition, dictates ministry style.

- The churches know about different groups in the community, and they design strategies accordingly.

- The churches work diligently to assimilate new people and help them feel at home at various stages along the entry path.

Chapter 7

Running the Race: Goals, Plans, and Organization

"The kings of the Gentiles lord it over them; and those who exercise authority over them call themselves Benefactors. But you are not to be like that. Instead, the greatest among you should be like the youngest, and the one who rules like the one who serves. For who is greater, the one who is at the table or the one who serves? Is it not the one who is at the table? But I am among you as one who serves. You are those who have stood by Me in My trials. And I confer on you a kingdom, just as My Father conferred one on me, so that you may eat and drink at My table in My kingdom and sit on thrones, judging the twelve tribes of Israel."

Luke 22:25–30

The churches we studied operate with planned, intentional ministries. Ministries are proactive and environment-shaping rather than reactive and environmentally responsive. They run the race to win the prize. They work to meet the goals of mission and ministry—saving souls—where the Lord has called them.

These churches actively set goals. Planning and goal-setting can be founded on human management or manipulative gimmicks, but in these courageous churches they were spiritual exercises.

Planning takes seriously stewardship of God's mysteries. It seeks to achieve the most from finite resources. Planning is motivated by a desire to be effective, and using resources effectively is good stewardship.

Goal-setting seeks the Lord's will, determines to declare and follow it, and monitors and evaluates progress toward accomplishing it.

The churches in this study committed themselves to running the race and to the choices, planning, and structures necessary for it.

Encouraging Intense Commitment

Showing courage, these churches call for high commitment from "average" lay people as well as from the leadership. At Immanuel in Palatine, IL, Pastor Theodore Eisold says, "Planning the services is a major effort each week. Further, I think the leadership now plans much better for [other] events, sometimes planning one year in advance for outside speakers and music groups. This ensures quality. Also, evaluation is present and important. Evaluation and adjustments along the way help us to make what we're doing better. There's a growing insistence on excellence in how we present ourselves—from ushers, elders, right down the line—to give the impression of excellence and caring throughout the service and the atmosphere of Sunday morning."

Pastor Raymond Cummings in Walden, NY, recounts, "First we began developing a biblical eldership, and the eldership gradually influenced the church council. This led to the selection of all our leaders with spiritual qualifications in mind. For example, we began to choose men who gave evidence of involvement in Bible study, solid home life, and understanding of the mission of the church."

The Rev. John Kieschnick at Gloria Dei in Houston, TX, expresses a similar commitment: "We raised the 'expectation level' of our leadership first and then that of our membership. All potential leaders were told that if they accepted their positions, they would worship, commune, and attend Bible class every Sunday unless the Lord prevented them." Kieschnick says raising expectations for leaders makes it easier to raise the entire congregation's commitment by requiring *all* prospective members to attend a 13-week new-member class. "Ninety percent of the time it's received very well. The 10 percent of the time it's not received well is usually among people who weren't active in their previous congregations. It seems that sometimes these are people who never came to grips with what a Christian commitment is. [When] they protested, I said, 'Then go to another church. We're not the only body of Christ around, but this is the way we define our ministry. We're not saying you're not a Christian. All we're saying is that to belong to this covenant community, there are certain expectations we have of one another, and we believe they're biblical.' We have few people that haven't joined—frankly, very few. At least those who join know what they're getting into."

Pastor Ingo Dutzmann of Redeemer in Cape Elizabeth, ME, believes that commitment to excellence includes commitment to biblical teaching and that the Lutheran Confessions are fundamental to help people understand clearly the truth of God's Word. Growth research during the past two decades substantiates that people seek doctrinal integrity on the basic issues of meaning, identity, and purpose. Many studies prove that churches certain about what they believe, teach, and practice attract people. People find no satisfaction in churches that seem to say "It doesn't matter what you believe, as long as you're sincere." They want a church with theological backbone and real meaning, a church that knows what it stands for and stands for what it knows.

Financial giving marks the high commitment at Our Savior in Centereach, NY. Pastor Ronald Stelzer says, "I challenge people with the tithe. I realize that a lot of people are in a situation where they cannot tithe. We don't explain the tithe in a legalistic way. But, in Old Testament times, the tithe was standard. I don't think God sent His Son, Jesus Christ, to encourage us to cut back—but to go forward!"

Stelzer says the impact on the congregation has been "tremendous." More money can build more ministry and increase staff. He believes high commitment to finances allows the church to grow. It's "not growth at any price, but Great Commission type growth. The Great Commission is our theme. The people have grown spiritually," Stelzer adds. "They've grown to realize that God is faithful, because, as Malachi 3:10 says, Put Him to the test. If you don't challenge people in the area of money, then you're leaving their idols intact and you'll never really make the breakthrough you need to make."

At Prince of Peace in Carrollton, TX, the congregation carried its commitment expectations into small-group ministry. "The philosophy behind the cell groups is very simple," explains the Rev. Stephen Wagner. "It's the issue of growing in your discipleship. It means that people are encouraged to grow in what it means to follow Christ, and it provides an opportunity for developing an accountability for that growth."

The high commitment level of Salem in Orange, CA, influenced how the church began its day school in a yuppie community. "The school needed to be prestigious with an outstanding reputation," explains Pastor Meyer. Therefore, the school offers a full computer wing as well as music and drama lessons. Upper grades learn Spanish. And the community prizes the school's full athletic program. Salem Church considers the school its "ripe harvest."

High commitment and expectations grow as a church plants other congregations. Lamb of God in Humble, TX, recently planted a church in Kingwood. Pastor John Miller explains that, because of Lamb of God's high commitment, "Within two months they [the Kingwood people] were supporting themselves. It's a congregation that puts high expectations on people before they're allowed to become members. You just can't walk in and join this congregation. And this is really working out, because people tend to come in [to the Kingwood church] with a high level of commitment, and they follow through on that. It's really exciting to see this."

Pastor Richard Elseroad of Good Shepherd in Gardendale, AL, summarizes commitment as theological. "Our church is serious about the Christian faith, about this idea of 'church,' of doing the Lord's work and doing it together. I believe the Lord has provided this commitment."

Offering Excellent Choices

When leaders design their church's ministries, some view the task as an either-or matter: "We can do this or that, but not both." Those we interviewed for this study see the church's ministry as a both-and dynamic. These leaders provide choices. They recognize the different needs among members and community people as well as the fact that everyone's needs vary from day to day. Therefore, these courageous church leaders do not "lock in" to any one view.

Consider, for example, how these churches deal with the tension about church nurseries. Mothers of small children in the 1990s want expert care in a clean, safe nursery near the sanctuary while they worship with their husbands and older children. Those who raised their children 15 to 20 years ago wonder why today's young mothers seem unable or unwilling to teach their small children church etiquette while cultivating the habit of attendance at the worship service. Churches with a both-and mentality understand, acknowledge,

125

accept, and meet the needs of both types of mother.

Most of these churches also recognize the different degrees of spiritual maturity and growth in discipleship among their members, and they offer appropriate learning experiences for all levels.

Traditional boards and committees do not lend themselves to offering choices. Rather than electing someone to an education committee and assuming (for example) that he or she is interested in every aspect of education (which may or may not be true), these churches emphasize specific ministries to which individuals are called.

One person may be good at organizing the educational facilities. Another may be called to a ministry of teaching specifically six-year-olds. Providing educational choices may also mean repeating experiences. For example, a church may provide the same spiritual gifts workshop annually. New members might participate at the first opportunity. Long-term members who have not taken it may be interested later. People change. Also, people who attended the previous year speak positively about the experience and increase interest among others.

Pastor Ronald Zehnder of St. Luke in Ann Arbor, MI, says a key element of change leading to growth is "unity in diversity" among the people.

At Trinity in Lisle, IL, Pastor Arthur Beyer and his people faced facility limitations because land was not available to plant more churches. They challenged themselves: How could they provide more worship and training opportunities *and* develop more small-group ministries? How could they better serve ethnic and special age groups? Would satellite operations in homes or rented facilities work? By moving beyond either-or thinking that would bind them to either "build here or move the church there," they discovered the many creative choices around them.

First Church in Charlotte, MI, demonstrated choice mentality in staffing. Though wanting to call a minister of assimilation, they realized their limited finances wouldn't allow them to bring in a professional church worker. By advertising in the congregation, a recent transfer showed a strong interest and background in this ministry. The pastor was especially grateful that this first staff addition happened to be a woman. He felt some people would feel more comfortable talking to her and that would be an asset.

Atonement in Glendale, AZ, emphasizes choices in lay involvement. "We strive to get as many people as possible working in various areas of the church in terms of committees, boards, and other responsibilities," says Pastor Ronald Kudick.

Providing multiple worship services forcefully demonstrates a church's choice mentality. Many congregations offer services at more than one time slot. First Church at Charlotte, MI, offers a Thursday evening worship service during the summer for vacationers, shift workers, and those working on Sunday mornings. But other reasons as well prompt choices. Among these courageous churches, 45 percent offer at least one contemporary worship service, and 73 percent offer variety within the regular worship service. Another 57 percent blend traditional and contemporary styles. Very few churches with more than one worship service keep identical styles.

In planning worship, the Rev. Edwin Doepel follows the "Baskin-Robbins" principle—Cross of Christ, Chattanooga, TN, didn't grow by serving just one flavor of ice cream. He describes the early service as very liturgical and the second one as "semicontemporary," with more alternatives. Pastor Jeffrey King of Christ in Southwick, MA, observes, "Our most popular service is our contemporary service."

Most of these churches offer choice in Bible study—in time, content, and leadership. "In addition to two or three Sunday morning offerings for adults, we have groups meeting on Monday, Wednesday, Thursday, and Friday mornings, as well as Wednesday evenings," said one pastor. King of Kings in San Antonio, TX, grew from one to seven Bible studies on Sunday mornings, plus additional weekly and monthly studies.

Surveying the data reveals that most of these churches offer programs ranging from low-commitment, topical discussions to high-commitment, long-term studies such as LifeLight, the Bethel Bible series, or Crossways.

This multiple-choice thinking helps these courageous churches reach people who live in a time-conscious society. They provide opportunities for people to find a group and topic appropriate to their level of commitment and spiritual maturity. This typifies unity in diversity—one teaching and doctrine, but diversified styles and opportunities.

127

Planning for Great Goals

These courageous churches plan not only for next month but next year. Most live by 5-year plans, and many think about the next 10 years and beyond. Growing churches recognize that change takes time. Nevertheless, their plans do not tyrannize these churches. They consider their plans a servant, not a master. They allow themselves freedom to change as they monitor and evaluate progress.

Because these churches plan for the long-term, most pastors indicate their commitment to long-term pastorates. This creates an evolving corporate mentality and allows churches to move beyond the daily maintenance and temporal changes accompanying short-term ministry.

Long-term planning provides for transformation. Long-term planning means churches realistically strategize for church planting, building a megachurch, developing a philosophy of ministry, establishing a reputation for youth ministry, expanding a ministry of music, developing a strong Christian school, or supporting a missionary family for their entire career on the mission field.

The Rev. John Frerking at Faith in North Palm Beach, FL, says that one of their priorities involves a systematic program of annual planning and goal-setting by church leaders.

Resurrection in Cary, NC, says its master plan allows the church to focus tasks toward the overall direction of its ministry.

When Chandler, AZ, a city of 25,000 near Phoenix, experienced in the early 1980s a spurt of rapid growth—retirees as well as young families—Epiphany Church there called Pastor Larry Stoterau in 1983. Church leaders wanted continued growth (the church already had contributed 30 members to launch Christ Church in Gilbert, AZ), and Stoterau's track record in a previous church proved his capacity for it. They seemed an ideal match.

The catch came when members felt the implications, the side effects, of continued growth. Stoterau had set the goal of stepping out in faith—in both programs and building projects, which meant that his role was changing as he became less of a "family chaplain" and more an administrator. Several key leaders grew uncomfortable with that and strongly criticized Stoterau for being too forceful. As Stoterau considered a call to another congregation, his Board of Elders chairman told him, "You always have a vision for us, and you shoot for it. Sometimes your vision is a little too far ahead of us; sometimes it's far out ahead of us, and we can't see that far."

Part of Stoterau's vision from the beginning was that worship be a positive and uplifting experience done with enthusiasm. Both Stoterau and his wife spend a lot of time coordinating the music and worship for the three Sunday morning services. Another vision that's materialized is a strong, well-established preschool and child care program. Besides strengthening current efforts, Stoterau supports continued growth in several ways. He wants to expand the staff with a director of assimilation and perhaps an evangelist later. The church is considering buying four acres of land to expand further. Soon they'll decide when and how to spin off a new mission to the south.

In order to plan for these great goals, the church uses a professional corporate consultant to guide them. Yet, Stoterau stresses, the members own the goals. They developed a five-year plan after the church consultant analyzed their congregation. Stoterau says, "Over the past six years, we've operated with too many short-term goals and too few long-term goals. Members haven't always caught the vision because they haven't seen the long-term effect. We've now developed a five-year plan, and I'd do that much earlier next time. Additionally, such a plan would involve and include a cross-representation of the congregation in addition to the existing leadership."

At Prince of Peace, Carrollton, TX, five-year goals include adding three new staff (visitation, music, athletics), increasing small groups from 30 to 40, adding a third Sunday school hour and two more worship hours, planting a daughter church, adding a development office, expanding a counseling center, and beginning a capital fund campaign for a new sanctuary. "The Lord's people should be given the opportunity to rise to the occasion, and you want to hold out a large vision for them," declares Pastor Wagner. "To hold out a large goal gets large response. You have a higher risk of failure when you hold up smaller goals than when you hold up larger ones. To do what we're planning is going to require some energy and careful planning, and there will be some pain involved. But that's what you get when you grow. I would rather deal with problems of growth than problems of plateauing and declining."

Some churches experience an anticlimactic lull, a "postpartum depression," after a building or church-planting project. Rev. Glenn Brauer says that Tallmadge Church in Tallmadge, OH, used goal-setting to move them through that period. Planning turned their eyes toward mission when they were tempted to "rest" and become maintenance-oriented. After the new building's dedication, they formed a vision committee to identify needs and goals for the next 5 to 10 years.

Pastor Dennis Kastens says Good Shepherd in Collinsville, IL, keeps focused on mission by involving leaders in a number of master-plan committees.

Pastor David Gohn organizes an annual planning retreat for leaders of Community in Flat Rock, MI.

Pastor Edwin Doepel of Cross of Christ Church in Chattanooga, TN, says, "I like a five-year plan because I like to shoot way down the road. That type of planning really pays off. It provides tremendous support from people, and congregational members can plan their lives around it. We had a Dialog Evangelism clinic one year with 150 people in attendance. We had such a large response because we started publicizing it a year ahead of time." When the church acquired a minicomputer, they converted to a major office system overnight. "That turned us around," Doepel believes. "People started catching the spirit that we need to keep moving on. Our office is very, very advanced now." Upgrading the office attracted a very capable assistant to oversee church administration. The church's long-range plans now include a larger sanctuary, more staff, training, and specialized ministries.

Some courageous churches adopt specific numerical goals. The late Pastor Dennis Schiefelbein, in Corpus Christi, TX, shared theirs. "We want to be over 1,000 members by 1993–94, and we're working for that. We're in the final phase of improving our Wednesday family night ministry and worship service. We have set a goal of 75 percent of our Sunday attendance at an average Wednesday service."

Trinity, Lisle, IL, committed itself to be a growing church when it built two additions in the 1970s, mostly to accommodate the increased Bible study. Another level of growth began in the early 1980s after Pastor Arthur Beyer's involvement in church-growth seminars and a doctor of ministry program. Next he educated and involved the leaders and the congregation in general in principles of growth, using books, films, and courses, such as the *Master's Plan* and *Your*

Church Can Grow. After the lay people solidly committed themselves to growth principles, Beyer then worked to expand leadership with the highest qualified staff members. The church's 10-year growth goals determine the annual goals, which are shared with the congregation. The growth in worship attendance slowed in 1988 during a construction year, but jumped 25 percent in 1989. Now the greatest barrier to continued growth is limited parking.

This monumental change in programs and size caused Beyer to develop greater administrative skills, which he purposefully learned through management courses and seminars. Because the majority of lay leaders are managers or work with management, they're comfortable with this arrangement. They view the pastor as chief executive officer, and they have "recognized" that view in their new constitution. Beyer has but one regret after 20 years. "I should have pushed harder to acquire more property and build bigger earlier on. We could have met the challenge. I lacked the vision at that time."

Lamb of God's staff in Humble, TX, constantly motivate members with dreams and plans. Pastor John H. Miller is encouraging the Futures Committee of 35 people to plan for a Christian day-care center, a sports complex to attract community members, a counseling service, and more classrooms and staff. Miller says he anticipates the congregation growing as large as possible on its current site, to about 1,200 communicants, and then planting other congregations.

The Rev. Elmer Thyr of Shepherd of the Hills in Rancho Cucamonga, CA, calls planning and goal setting fundamental for a new church. In fact, he says, "Every decision in the beginning bears on the future personality of the church. The beginning nucleus and all subsequent members should be taught to assume the church will become a large congregation."

A preacher's ability sets the course, Thyr explains. "We're responsible to do our best. And if our best creates a church of 1,000 or 2,000, praise the Lord. If our best efforts simply maintain a modest church of 250—as long as we're faithful, that's all we can be called upon to do. But if we have the ability to have a church of 1,000 and we're satisfied with a church of 200 and we don't do those things necessary to attract those people who aren't Christians and who need the Gospel—then we've got problems."

Organizing Pragmatically

Like the farmer who plants many seeds, the leaders in our study recognize their responsibility to cultivate and harvest. They aim for results, to bear much fruit. They desire effective ministries. They passionately seek achievement of goals and celebrate victories. Therefore, they operate with a pragmatic ministry. They're able to separate essentials from nonessentials. Identifying nonessentials, which Protestant forefathers called "adiaphora," dynamically recaptures the Reformation's spirit and power. When the Christian church in any age confuses what can change with what cannot change, it loses some authenticity, relevance, and power—and may grow anemic in providing a clear path for the Gospel to travel in its contemporary setting. Consequently, operating pragmatically adds to the mix making these churches truly orthodox and genuinely Christian.

Pastor Bradley Hoefs represents this balance well when he describes the mission statement of large King of Kings, Omaha, NE. "We have a mindset to be true to the Word of God. We're going to be conservative doctrinally, teaching only what the Bible teaches. But we will be progressive and innovative as we teach. We will be traditional in doctrine but nontraditional in carrying out the ministry. We are not afraid to take the doctrine and package it in a new way."

Hoefs is pragmatic in his role as senior pastor. He says, "There's probably a lot more that I don't even know about. There's a price you have to pay for being a senior pastor. I just read a book on 13 fatal errors that managers make. And I'm so gifted, I was making all 13 at one time! One [error] is thinking [that] when you're in charge, when you're the boss so to speak, that people will trust you 100 percent. It's just not going to be that way on this side of heaven."

Pastor Christopher Dodge at St. Matthew in Walled Lake, MI, demonstrates "holy pragmatism," too. "We believe that if something's not working, then it's time to find something different," he says simply. "If it means doing something no one else has tried before, it's certainly worth a shot. The worst we can do is have it not work, learn from our losses and go from there to find something better."

Pastor Barrie Henke of Shepherd of the Hills in Onalaska, WI, echoes, "We'll try it; and if it works, fine. We'll praise God for it! If it doesn't work, we'll quit doing it. We'll do something else. That's always been our very aggressive attitude. I've always considered myself flexible and willing to try different things." When asked if he was a risktaker, Henke replied, "I'd say so; I'm in the ministry!"

This pragmatism originates from a desire to meet people's needs. Pastor Richard Meyer of Lawton, OK, discusses worship based on need. "It depends on the community. If the community is within a weekend reach to resorts or lakes, then Saturday night may not be a good time for a worship service because people are gone for the whole weekend. So Thursday night or Monday night tends to be better. The main thing is to do whatever works."

Pragmatism relates also to worship style. Pastor Elmer Thyr in Rancho Cucamonga, CA, describes the first step of his pilgrimage to pragmatism. "What contemporary services meant to me initially," he says, "was that I left out 'thees' and 'thous.' It evolved into a deliberate attempt both from the pulpit and the printed liturgy to speak in such a way that the unchurched knew what we were talking about. I've been doing that now for 25 years."

For Prince of Peace, Carrollton, TX (as well as a number of congregations in our study), organizing pragmatically meant leaving behind a "single-cell" structure in favor of a staff-driven polity that enables courageous ministry. When the Rev. Stephen Wagner came in 1978, the church consisted of 300 members, with basic decisions made at a monthly voters' assembly meeting. When the church grew from one to two worship services, a parish planning council of 15 leaders made basic decisions, and the voters' assembly met once a quarter and elected council members. After a recent year-long effort to study and rewrite the constitution and bylaws, goal-setting, decision-making, and vision-casting now rests mostly with the staff. The congregation has a 10-person board of directors, and the voters' assembly meets just twice a year. The staff develops proposals and submits them to the board. Daily decision-making thus rests in the hands of the most informed people—the staff, which selects and equips the lay members and leaders to carry out the church's various ministries and activities. The system places less emphasis on who is in control and more on everyone's pursuing ministry opportunities as they emerge.

Good Shepherd's school in Collinsville, IL, grew from working cooperatively with a nearby Christian day school to operating its own school with an independent enrollment of 500 in just 10 years; regular church attendance nearly tripled. So much change and growth in church and school often creates congregational tensions and even resistance—but not at Good Shepherd. The church expects program development to come from the staff, particularly the pastors. Yet no formal congregational decision occurs until staff extensively explores and discusses the program with those concerned. They identify potential barriers in advance and bring them into open forums. By this approach, decisions are virtually unanimous. Kastens acknowledges he's spending more time on administration and less on member calls, but he feels that if he abandons the administrative load, then growth results will not last because people won't stay around. Unspectacular, steady growth is much better, he says. [More pragmatic, we'd add.]

Strong leaders adapt and modify their ministry style as congregations grow. Dr. Richard Lessmann, senior pastor at Grace in Huntsville, AL, explains: "As the ministry became more complex, including additional personnel, my job description changed to the point where I function now in the capacity of a 'rancher.' We're no longer a small church where I can be in personal contact with most of the members. The transition was somewhat strained. It's hard for some folks to accept that you can't run a large church with a small-church mentality."

The Rev. Paul Moldenhauer of First Church, Charlotte, MI, also found organizational change to be pragmatic. The congregation, he says, didn't "have a makeup that's tied to any tradition of what a church may or may not be. They may not go for some off-the-wall stuff, but . . . if there's a better way we can serve the Lord and minister to God's people, they're willing to go for it."

Pastor Moldenhauer stresses how much a church-growth seminar on "Breaking the 200 Barrier" helped him. Using Lyle Schaller's categories, he saw four distinct phases in the past 15 years of the congregation's history. In the first phase, under a previous pastor, the church grew from a fellowship to a "small church." Worship attendance grew from 64 to a church-filled 140. The second phase, from "small" to "middle-sized" church, occurred between 1981 and 1985. When Moldenhauer came in 1981, he added a second service to overcome space limitations and completed a new facility in 1984. He also developed an appropriate infrastructure to support more relationships: a board of evangelism in 1981, home Bible study groups in 1982, a board of Christian care in 1984, a board of fellowship in 1985, and a new constitution in 1985 that transferred ministry decisions from the voters' assembly to a church council. This resulted in a most difficult time for pastor and church. The surface question was whether to begin a preschool; but real underlying issues involved shifting to "maintenance ministry" for a while and assessing the appropriateness of the pastor's "rancher" style of ministry (that is, enabling members to visit, care, and minister to each other). The congregation approved the preschool start and Moldenhauer's ministry style by a 60 percent vote. Eventually several key leaders opposing it left. Moldenhauer says losing those leaders was the toughest time for him.

The third phase occurred when First Church "broke the 200 barrier" (1986–88). Key changes in structure and program included spiritual gifts and stewardship programs, annual evaluation and planning, a third summer service, and adding more office staff. Moldenhauer received confirmation of successfully moving through this stage when a member said, "You know, we're doing so much stuff around here, Pastor, that I can't even go to everything." The church, once a one-cell family, had become a multicelled church.

The fourth phase, moving beyond 200 to an "awkward-sized" church, began in 1989 when the congregation added a part-time assimilation coordinator and expanded the parking lot and educational wing.

Reflecting on his experience, Moldenhauer offers, "I've learned a lot about visioning and strategizing. It's important to have a variety of opportunities. You can only run one program so long, and then you have to bring in something fresh. Our whole infrastructure needs programmatic offerings for better ministry to our people, and for outreach. I have to provide a style of pastoral leadership there. And I have learned to be more concerned about 'majoring on the major issues' instead of majoring in some of the minor matters that really don't impact the growth or health of the church, or that lay leaders could have done just as well or better than I."

Some churches, like St. John, Glendale, NY, recognized the need for radical change in organizational structure. The church moved from a democracy with voters' assembly and church council to the "body-life" concept of a board of appointed elders.

135

The Rev. Arthur Beyer, the pastor of Trinity in Lisle, IL, talks about his life-cycle changes in style. "As the church grew even larger, I needed even greater administrative skills. I found that need satisfied through graduate study and, specifically, management courses, and seminars. The lay leadership felt comfortable with this style since the majority of the congregation is managerial or work in that situation.

"We're just now moving into the fourth level, a large church with a multiple staff. Our style is moving in the direction of more authority and decision-making in the hands of staff, less meetings for laity, and more hands-on ministry [by all]. The pastor is viewed more as a CEO. The new constitution will probably reflect these changes."

How did these pastors learn how to lead a larger church? Usually by trial and error, reading books, attending seminars, and learning through experience.

Perspective

According to an organizational style greatly advocated in the 1960s—"participative management"—a church should attempt to involve as many people as possible in decision-making. The more people who process the decision, the more committed they become and the more ownership they take in goal fulfillment. However, as membership in a congregation increases, so do the complications and the amount of energy needed to gain widespread participation. Committees compound the process when "checking" with others—which consumes more time and involvement. At some point, the growing church offers so many programs and activities that volunteer officers and leaders can no longer manage them without considerable time and effort. Growth adds complications and is perceived as a burden.

Spending so much effort on process leaves little time or energy for hands-on ministry and implementation. Creating a smaller number of policy boards with wider responsibilities is a natural progression for growing churches. Overall member participation in daily decision-making decreases. At the same time, energy to implement ministry increases as larger numbers of members receive training to carry out substantive ministry, while being relieved of "busy work."

In the story of Immanuel, Palatine, IL, the senior pastor wished to use his gifts in other areas than administration. He switched to an associate role, and the congregation called a senior pastor from outside the congregation.

Prince of Peace in Carrollton, TX, and Good Shepherd in Collinsville, IL, demonstrate another step. They've become essentially staff-led churches with something like a board of directors representing the congregation and reacting to staff proposals. Such representatives do not initiate programs.

Reorganization may be needed also because a congregation's growth inevitably increases the number of relationships possible between participants and especially between pastor and members. With small numbers, those relationships happen somewhat spontaneously and informally. But relying on such dynamics becomes hazardous for churches aspiring to grow beyond the convenient "family" size. Without an appropriate organizational structure to shape and guide relationships, continuing growth becomes more and more difficult.

No one organizational plan can provide a framework facilitating the best functioning for all sizes. Generally, four sizes with distinct organization emerge. Highlighting the pastor's role in each, they are (1) the pastor as family chaplain; (2) the pastor as organization with almost all church events and activities centered on the pastor's initiative and sustaining effort; (3) the pastor with organization where the lay leadership exercises more oversight in partnership with the pastor and a great deal more involvement in hands-on ministry; and (4) the pastor with staff serving a large church, providing a staff-led ministry with very high member participation. This staff usually includes key congregational lay leaders and executives along with professional church workers. The rest of the organization usually gets streamlined so people are free to minister.

Struggling to change and refine their church's structure constantly challenges leaders of growing churches. If they do not create appropriate solutions, they face two outcomes: (1) leaders burned out from keeping the organizational apparatus moving; or (2) growth self-pruned to a size fitting the current structure.

In summary, these courageous churches model modern cor-

137

porations, with a church executive officer being responsible to a single board. Taking such a courageous step tests the comfortable limits of many pastors and most congregations.

Let's again review some of the principles for sustaining growth discussed in chapter 1:

- Congregational leaders communicate high expectations for members. People feel strongly committed to the work of ministry in the congregation. Members place the church as a high priority in their lives.

- The churches operate from a worldview that offers choice—in Bible studies, service times, and worship styles.

- These churches plan. The professional and lay leaders set goals and work toward fulfillment of them.

- The leaders of these churches organize pragmatically, display a passion for success and effectiveness, and celebrate goals achieved as victories.

- The churches sustain growth by change in the organizational relationship between pastor and people, in the structures of congregational decision-making, and in continued self-analysis and redefinition of the ministry philosophy, frequently with the aid of church consultants.

Chapter 8

Am I Courageous? Can Our Church Become Courageous?

"I am the vine; you are the branches. If a man remains in Me and I in him, he will bear much fruit; apart from Me you can do nothing. If anyone does not remain in Me, he is like a branch that is thrown away and withers; such branches are picked up, thrown into the fire and burned. If you remain in Me and My words remain in you, ask whatever you wish, and it will be given you. This is to My Father's glory, that you bear much fruit, showing yourselves to be My disciples. . . . My command is this: Love each other as I have loved you. Greater love has no one than this, that he lay down his life for his friends. You are My friends if you do what I command. . . . You did not choose Me, but I chose you and appointed you to go and bear fruit—fruit that will last. Then the Father will give you whatever you ask in My name. This is My commandment: Love each other."

John 15:5–17

This book shares the stories of God-given courage in the church. Not all of the churches are wildly successful. Not all their actions produced marvelous results. The pastors who completed our questionnaires and who participated in the interview probably would not claim outstanding courage. Nevertheless, readers knowledgeable in congregational affairs probably found themselves saying about some of the stories, "Well, *that* certainly took a bit of courage!"

Everyone admires people of courage; we seek heroes. We want to view ourselves as courageous, even though we all harbor the nagging fear that someone (our spouse, children, congregation, friends, colleagues) will discover the many small or large cowardices that clutter up the closets of our lives—despair, defensiveness, resentment, disparagement. So we place a high value on courageous action.

But we come back to the question at the beginning of this book: What makes some churches courageous? And, why some and not others? Ultimately: Is it possible for *my* church to become courageous, to learn courage?

Without debating theoretical explanations, it seems more helpful to search for commonalities among these samples. What did they do or have that produced a courageous approach to the church's task in their particular place?

Courageous Pastors

The anecdotal evidence seems key and impressive. Unless a pastor clearly provides courageous leadership, there is little likelihood that any significant, effective ministry happens. If the shepherd runs or hides when wolves of any kind appear, we can not really expect a flock to counterattack. However, not all courageous pastors will produce courageous congregations. Recalcitrant lay leaders may refuse to accept strong pastoral leadership or accept change. Or the pastor may not use the best pastoral wisdom and tact, or show sufficient love of people. So how does a pastor develop a courageous leadership style that does work? The pastors we studied provided insight about themselves, about courageous leaders.

Courageous leaders possess some common characteristics:

1. They are people of conviction, and conviction gives birth to courage. In all our research material, not one leader voiced a single doubt about the veracity and dependability of Scripture or its power to move the heart. They were devoted to its message.

Not one leader voiced a single doubt about the Gospel, its reality and its power. Some spoke freely about their own conversion experience as a startling and determinative event in their lives.

Ample evidence shows they maintain a towering trust in God's power and leading. They have strong faith, even during discouraging setbacks.

They also feel conviction about their purpose. They know God has placed them where they are in order to fulfill the Lord's mission to reach the lost and lead them to the Savior.

2. They are people of passion. Leaders devote wholehearted attention to their goals and purpose. Their singleness of mind sometimes seems almost frightening. They may not always wear their passion on their sleeves, but you recognize in them an awesome sense of urgency; they want to succeed—now—and with all their hearts.

They are consumed with passion for their work. That passion calls forth courageous decisions and actions, heedless of obstacles.

3. They are people of vision. What these leaders dream about for the congregation is truly exciting, whether it be a Christian day school, a retreat camp, a day-care center, a Sunday attendance of more than 1,000, or expanded sites and facilities for ministry. Dreams abound—and they are no small dreams.

Nor are they idle daydreams. These future-oriented leaders can clearly articulate what their congregations will be like 10 or 20 years from now and can excite others in that vision. The dreams loom so large that temporary setbacks do not frustrate them.

Vision grants courage.

4. They are people of knowledge. These leaders analyze their congregations and communities, identify what barriers hamper mission, and decide what must be done to have the congregations flourish. They know about various programs and how to select among them.

They know how to bring about intentional change, making use of timing and finesse. Of course, they would not survive long without that capacity.

Furthermore, they know how to manage conflict. They are neither afraid of nor intimidated by conflict. They resolve it, one way or another.

And finally, they know how to motivate people—how to stimulate them to worship, to study, to serve, to witness, to give.

They know these matters, and they know that they know them. That gives them a confidence approaching seeming arrogance at times. They know they are competent at their craft, and that gives them courage.

Most constantly attend seminars on church methods and people skills, and avidly read books and journals dealing with administration, conflict, staffing, or new approaches in evangelism, motivation, and church growth. They eagerly seek to learn more from others.

The knowledge they gain fosters confidence and courage.

5. They are people of prayer. Leaders practice an active prayer life. Not many claim to intercede for hours at a time, but they evidently know how to storm the gates of heaven with fervent prayer. They say they depend on it.

Some surround themselves with (or are surrounded by) prayer circles. These leaders find strength in knowing that the people regularly pray for their protection, wisdom and insight.

In prayer they take courage.

6. They are people open to affirmation. Here we have an anomaly. On one hand, these leaders are, or give the impression of being, very confident, secure, and self-assured. They are quite independent in action, and not particularly concerned about getting official permission for what they do. On the other hand, they feel offended and disappointed at times when they think their ministry is misunderstood and "suspect" by their peers in ministry and/or denominational officials. They will network with like-minded pastors (at times, those of other denominations) for support, and so find encouragement.

So then, these courageous leaders derive courage from their convictions, passion, vision, knowledge and affirmation from colleagues. Most of them feel pride in their congregations, and are eager to move them to a greater level of ministry. Most like being where they are, and feel affirmed, appreciated, and effective.

Courageous Laity

Lay leaders were highly visible in all the churches we studied. They helped their congregation be courageous. Their role was as follows:

1. Welcome and support a rich Word and Sacrament environment, including the Bible-based study of God's will for a congregation, in Bible classes, sermons, board and committee meetings, and organization devotions so that God's Word firmly establishes the conviction of the congregation.

2. Participate in periodic evangelism training sessions and relational skill development forums to enhance understanding and competence in ministry. If they are not being offered, take the initiative to sponsor them.

3. Expect and encourage other congregational leaders to attend conferences on churchmanship (administration, conflict management, small-group life, mercy ministries, education, creative staffing, publicity, church growth, and the like).

4. Encourage each other to high expectations in living out a Christian corporate and individual life.

5. Schedule at least one victory celebration each month, with perhaps one large annual celebration of accomplishments and accomplishers.

6. Work and pray together to fashion and adopt an exciting vision for the future.

7. Expect and encourage other congregational leaders to read and study timely books and journals on effective church growth methods.

8. Provide prayer groups to pray for the pastor and other leaders, for the congregation's future, and for faithful obedience to the Lord's will for your church.

These enhance courage—developing a base of conviction, assembling ministry skills, promoting an environment of high expectations, celebrating positive events, and praying. This is by no means an exhaustive list of ways laity nourish the development of courageous churches. But it is derived from the experience of churches in our survey.

Courageous Action: The Process of Unfreezing, Change, and Refreezing

Social psychologists talk about three phases in the change process: unfreezing, change, and refreezing. Change can not happen until a person or group realizes that current action is no longer appropriate or functional. This is the "unfreezing" phase.

Some people's attitudes change when they no longer receive positive feedback. What once brought affirmation and congratulations now meets with indifference. Most people are not willing to change until they finally believe that their actions are resulting in negative consequences, which they too do not like.

Once people become "unfrozen" from their old methods, they can seriously consider alternatives, preferably several. Ultimately, they must chart a course and perspective to bring positive results.

As affirmative change occurs, new ways and attitudes are reinforced and eventually "frozen" again.

Grace in Bradford, PA, was ready for change. Members' attitudes were "unfrozen" when they acknowledged the very real prospect of closing. Getting ready for change involved finding new officers and a pastor.

Pastor J. Arthur Cox emphasized involving more people in Bible study. Buying and then remodeling the grocery store gave them a positive experience that overshadowed disappointments. Their increasing enthusiasm prepared them to take seriously their self-study. Their path to continued growth seems assured for the foreseeable future.

The Christians of St. John in Glendale, NY, certainly could not deny they were aging and had no young members to carry on. Neighborhood change was indisputable. Yet pastors who ministered to them in the 1970s encountered a pride that made change difficult. But when their pride broke, they found courage. They were "unfrozen" and prepared for Pastor Donald Miles' fresh initiatives. They could follow his leadership in renewing their identity and mission in Christ. They set a new, effective course.

In many ways, the unfreezing process resembles repentance before God. Churches and institutions, just like individuals, need to stay open to God's leading.

Courageous Action: Innovatively Moving beyond Tradition

In some respects the baby-boom generation lives in a different culture from its parents. Yet each denomination's outreach improves as the challenge of reaching other American subcultures becomes more obvious.

Lutheranism, in addition to its confessional theology, has its own culture which (as any denomination's culture) involves music, history, and symbols (including symbolic actions). The way Lutherans express that culture was formed originally in Germany and Scandinavia. And, at one point in America, a unified expression of that culture across the land served to identify Lutherans to each other as part of their homogeneous group. Part of Lutheranism's inherited culture places a high value on uniformity in church life. For many the ideal would be that all Lutheran churches throughout the country experience the same form of worship and church life so that as people transfer or visit they feel at home.

However, with the mobility and interactions of younger generations as they became assimilated in the 'stew pot' of American culture, time seems to be against a continued vitality of the traditional expressions of Lutheran culture. Neighborhoods newly dominated by Hispanic or Asian populations focus this challenge. Only as congregations bridge the gap between their cultural packaging of the Gospel of Jesus Christ and the culture of the new residents will those congregations continue to be effective.

Few congregations will face as much cultural diversity as St. Peter's in Brooklyn. But they will face increased diversity and change in some form, if only between generations.

How have churches responded? There is no one, pat answer. The most effective forms of ministry and outreach have been developed individually. Willingness to become innovative—to move beyond the conventional—is paramount. Pursuing such innovation takes courage, given by the Holy Spirit.

We don't mean that all churches must change everything they're doing. Many may enjoy the favorable circumstances of enough people in their communities who know and appreciate their inherited religious culture. If what they are doing yields a healthy, growing congregational life, then they should stay with it. Many congregations, however, do not enjoy spiritual and numerical growth. Church leaders are always challenged to recognize what cannot or need not be changed and to change what can and should be.

Courageous Action: What to Do

If any Christian wants to help his or her church be courageous, our study suggests the following:

1. Honestly examine your basic convictions about the Holy Scriptures, the Gospel's power and beauty, your trust in a powerful and accepting heavenly Father, and your ultimate purpose as Christ's servant.

2. Examine your passions. Are you more passionate about liturgical niceties, rectitude in doctrinal formulations, or absolute conformity with traditional administration forms than the salvation of souls? It takes passion to develop the courage to build great churches.

3. Spend time clarifying for yourself a great vision of your congregation's future. What is God waiting to bless among you? Let your vision be discerning and exceptional.

4. Develop a proficiency in church leadership and management and in people skills (conflict resolution, motivation, group dynamics, church growth, evangelism techniques, etc.) by attending seminars, reading books and journals, and visiting other thriving churches. Knowledge produces confidence, and that builds courage.

5. Examine your prayer life. Give God no rest (Is. 62:7), but remind Him of His promises. Ask prayer groups to intercede for you in your quest, either before or during the worship service or at other times.

6. Seek the support and encouragement of like-minded brothers and sisters in Christ. You will know them by their testimony and works. They will, with rare exceptions, value your encouragement as you cherish theirs.

Courageous Action: One Final Story

In conclusion, we share with you the story of a courageous church that puts into practice many of the principles presented in this book.

Mount Calvary was founded in 1941, when Beverly Hills was just another community within greater Los Angeles, and heavily Protestant.

By the early 1960s, the city's population had become Jewish— 97 percent, by some estimates. Mount Calvary, like most Protestant churches there, experienced a dramatic dip in membership, from 600 to a mere 45.

Just before Pastor R. John Perling arrived in Beverly Hills in May 1972, Mount Calvary's leaders were offered $1 million in cash in an attaché case for their property. Should they sell and relocate? Many other churches, three other Lutheran churches among them, already had left the area. Replacing the cross with the star of David proved too difficult a thought for them, and they turned down the offer. They would remain in the community as witnesses to Christ.

Perling, a lifelong Minnesota Lutheran whose heritage may well be Jewish, is an especially good fit for the Mount Calvary ministry; yet for the first five years of Perling's pastorate nothing of major consequence in Jewish evangelism happened. The Jews for Jesus movement already had a significant impact on the Jewish community and drew reaction. Then tension in this community rose dramatically when Perling and Mount Calvary were recognized as aggressive in evangelistic outreach to Jewish people, asserting that Jewish people were "incomplete" without Jesus Christ.

A new phase of mission began when Mount Calvary started its own facilities in what is now the largest Christian synagogue—the Messianic Synagogue—in the Los Angeles area. To celebrate this new ministry, a number of regional church leaders participated in a streetside building rededication.

Outreach to the community changed most dramatically after six rabbis visited Perling with demands. They did not mind Mount Calvary's presence, they insisted, but they strongly resented any outreach efforts, viewing them as a direct insult. Perling took them around and showed them the Messianic Synagogue and the liturgical books, which were identical to their own. "The chief difference of course is that Jesus Christ is the central figure of all synagogue worship. That is an offense to them, but Christ is the offense and not us. We have to make very sure that we keep that separate in the ministry. If we become the offense, then of course we miss the whole thing," Perling says.

Over the years, Mount Calvary and particularly the Messianic Synagogue have encountered threats and many acts of vandalism; however, these incidents increased people's awareness of their mission, especially among younger Christians. The Messianic Synagogue has experienced a large growth in membership and Mount Calvary a modest one. Spiritual growth has taken off in both congregations because of the challenge. The synagogue now numbers over 100 in worship and Mount Calvary has over 180 members with an average of 105 in worship.

Perling preaches for the Messianic Synagogue on occasion but they have their own spiritual leader, Rabbi Barry Budoff. "We are very close with our Christian synagogue people, and since we worship on different days we can often attend each other's worship services. The Rabbi and I are together a couple times a week and confer with each other regularly," Perling comments.

Advertising in the Beverly Hills paper aids their outreach. "Today our ad is right next to the ad by Jews for Judaism [a group organized to oppose missionary activity directed toward Jewish people] . . . in which they offer a course on the seven Wednesdays of our Lenten season," Perling notes as he considers the competition. "We also have opened our facilities to community groups. Three Jewish AA groups meet in the same hall as do the worshiping Jewish Christians—on different evenings."

The highly specialized mission outreach to Jews begins by emphasizing the common Old Testament heritage of both Jews and Christians. Observes Perling, "The trouble with a lot of missionary work among Jewish people is when the change [completion] comes, they try to remove all of the Jewish background. What we have to understand is that there is absolutely nothing going on in the Jewish synagogue that is anti-Christian, except that of leaving Christ out of it. But Jesus Christ is a very integral part of all those Jewish celebrations. He celebrated them Himself."

Members of both Mount Calvary and the Messianic Synagogue tell of many interesting stories of conversions and community relations, as well as interactions with movie stars. Rather than being cautious in their "unwelcomed" outreach, these people now have two full-time missionaries, Rabbi Steven Stern and Milton Kohut, to the Jewish population. They are a unique Christian presence in an area of Los Angeles County, where more than 100,000 people live.

This courageous church and pastor do not just survive in this area, which has little opportunity for conventional ministry. Mount Calvary's witness embraces Iranians moving into the community and other groups. Recently, they became "home" to a Korean congregation led by Rev. Du Pyo Lee that worships on Sunday afternoon. The three clergy, Perling, Budoff, and Lee share the facilities as they reach out with Christ to different ethnic groups. [More recently, Rev. Lee's Korean church was relocated in Riverside, CA, and a Hungarian Reformed congregation has moved in.]

Perling summarizes, "Our church has grown from a closed in, exclusive group to an outreaching, loving, expanding, sharing, concerned band of followers of Messiah-Jesus. They are familiar with the worship of Christian people different from themselves and are not frightened by it."

Perling dreams and plans on opening a Gentile bookstore and

discussion center in a heavily orthodox Jewish section. Perling joyously looks forward to sharing Christ even though he anticipates that "there will be a lot of confrontation going on down there because I'll be right in their back yard."

Perling regrets not being more aggressive in outreach earlier in his tenure. He admits he was unnecessarily reluctant to proceed rapidly, because he worried how church officials would perceive the ministry. "Once I didn't care anymore how they perceived the ministry," he says, "everything went well. Now [among my peers] I'm known as the 'Lutheran Rabbi' " . . . a fitting label for a courageous pastor.

May God grant all of us the courage to live in His will and in the power of the Spirit, to fulfill Christ's mandate to make disciples.

Participating Churches

Alabama

Good Shepherd Lutheran Church
2477 North Road
Gardendale, AL 35071
205/631-2355

Grace Lutheran Church
3321 S. Memorial Parkway
Huntsville, AL 35801-5396
205/881-0552

Alaska

Zion Lutheran Church
2112 McCullam Avenue
Fairbanks, AK 99701
907/456-7660

Arizona

Epiphany Lutheran Church
800 W. Ray Road
Chandler, AZ 85224
602/963-6105

Atonement Lutheran Church
4001 W. Beardsley Road
Glendale, AZ 85308
602/582-8785

Arkansas

Bethel Lutheran Church
5400 Euper Lane
Fort Smith, AR 72903
501/452-1521

California

Shepherd of the Hills Lutheran Church
Rancho Cucamonga
6080 Haven
Alta Loma, CA 91701
714/989-6500

St. John Lutheran Church
912 New Stine Road
Bakersfield, CA 93309
805/834-1412

Mount Calvary Lutheran Church
436 S. Beverly Drive
Beverly Hills, CA 90212
213/277-1164

Mount Olive Lutheran Church
65 Evans Road
Milpitas, CA 95035
408/262-0506

Salem Lutheran Church
19952 Santiago Canyon Road
Orange [Orange Park Acres], CA 92669
714/633-2366

Colorado

King of Kings Lutheran Church
8300 Pomona Drive
Arvada, CO 80005
303/425-7096

Florida

Faith Lutheran Church
555 US 1 and Ebbtide
North Palm Beach, FL 33408
407/848-4737

Redeemer Lutheran Church
2450 SE Ocean Boulevard
Stuart, FL 34996
407/287-0434

Georgia

Holy Cross Lutheran Church
377 Valley Hill Road, S.W.
Riverdale, GA 30274
404/478-9324

Illinois

Good Shepherd Lutheran Church
1300 Belt Line
Collinsville, IL 62234
618/344-3151

Trinity Lutheran Church
1101 Kimberly Way (Rt. 53)
Lisle, IL 60532
708/964-1272

Immanuel Lutheran Church
200 North Plum Grove Road
Palatine, IL 60067
708/359-1549

Indiana

Redeemer Lutheran Church
1811 Lincoln Avenue
Evansville, IN 47714
812/476-9991

Iowa

Trinity Lutheran Church
1122 West Central Park
Davenport, IA 52804
319/323-8001

Grace Lutheran Church
Box 156
De Witt, IA 52742
319/659-9153

Kansas

Immanuel Lutheran Church
2104 W. 15th
Lawrence, KS 66049-2105
913/843-0620

Maine

Redeemer Lutheran Church
126 Spurwink Avenue
Cape Elizabeth, ME 04107
207/799-5941

Massachusetts

Christ Lutheran Church
568 College Hwy, P.O. Box 1107
Southwick, MA 01077-1107
413/569-5151

Michigan

St. Luke Lutheran Church
4205 Washtenaw Road
Ann Arbor, MI 48108
313/971-0550

First Lutheran Church
550 E. Shepherd, Box 413
Charlotte, MI 48813-0413
517/543-4360

St. Mark Lutheran Church
1934 52nd Street SE
Kentwood, MI 49508
616/455-5320

Immanuel Lutheran Church
47120 Romeo Plank
Mount Clemens, MI 48044
313/286-4231

Faith Lutheran Church
37635 Dequindre
Troy, MI 48083
313/689-4664

St. Matthew Lutheran Church
2040 S. Commerce Road
Walled Lake, MI 48390
313/624-7676

Hope Lutheran Church
32400 Hoover Rd.
Warren, MI 48093
313/979-9055

Minnesota

Family of Christ Lutheran Church
16045 Nightingale Street, N.W.
Andover, MN 55304
612/434-7337

Missouri

King of Kings Lutheran Church
13765 Olive Boulevard
Chesterfield, MO 63017
314/469-2224

Nebraska

King of Kings Lutheran Church
2600 S. 124th Street
Omaha, NE 68144
402/333-6464

New York

Our Savior Lutheran Church
Mark Tree Road and Tree Road
Centereach, NY 11720
516/588-2757

St. John Lutheran Church
88-24 Myrtle Avenue
Glendale, NY 11385
718/847-3188

Trinity Lutheran Church
Route 208, Rd 2, Box 403A
Walden, NY 12586
914/778-7119

North Carolina

Resurrection Lutheran Church
2002 Kildaire Farm Road
Cary, NC 27511
919/851-7248

Ohio

Tallmadge Lutheran Church
759 East Avenue
Tallmadge, OH 44278
216/633-4775

Oklahoma

St. John Lutheran Church
Seventh and A Streets
Lawton, OK 73501
405/353-0556

Faith Lutheran Church
9222 N. Garnett Road
Owasso, OK 74055
918/272-9858

Pennsylvania

Grace Lutheran Church
79 Mechanic Street
Bradford, PA 16701
814/362-3244

Tennessee

Cross of Christ Lutheran Church
3204 Hixson Pike
Chattanooga, TN 37415
615/877-7447

Texas

Prince of Peace Lutheran Church
2115 Frankford Road
Carrollton, TX 75007
214/245-7564

Nuestro Salvador Lutheran Church
6102 Greenwood
Corpus Christi, TX 78417
512/857-5673

Gloria Dei Lutheran Church
18220 Upper Bay Road
Houston, TX 77058
713/333-4535

Lamb of God Lutheran Church
1400 Bypass 1960 East
Humble, TX 77338
713/446-8427

King of Kings Lutheran Church
13888 Dreamwood Drive
San Antonio, TX 78233
512/656-6508

Wisconsin

Emmaus Lutheran Church
2818 N. 23rd Street
Milwaukee, WI 53206
414/444-6090

Shepherd of the Hills Lutheran Church
Box 416
Onalaska, WI 54650
608/783-0330

Appendix II

Resources

1. Journals

Write for subscription information to the following:

Clergy Journal
P. O. Box 16527
Austin, TX 78716

Discipleship
P. O. Box 54470
Boulder, CO 80323-4470

Emerging Trends
P. O. Box 628
Princeton, NJ 08542

Global Church Growth
Church Growth Center
Corunna, IN 46730

Leadership
P. O. Box 8015
Wheaton, IL 60189-9815

McIntosh Church Growth Network
3630 Camellia Drive
San Bernardino, CA 92404

Ministries Today
P. O. Box 881
Farmingdale, NY 11737-9981

Net Results
5001 Avenue North
Lubbock, TX 74912

Win Arn Growth Report
2670 South Myrtle Avenue
Monrovia, CA 91016

2. Professional Lutheran Church Consultants

If your congregation is experiencing complex challenges, consider calling in a trained, experienced church consultant. You might want to contact:

The Rev. Paul T. Heinecke
Church Renewal Consultations
2464 Nixon Road
Ann Arbor, MI 48105

The Rev. Dr. Kent R. Hunter
Church Growth Center
Corunna, IN 46730

The Rev. Dr. John H. Miller
Lamb of God Lutheran Church
1400 Bypass 1960
Humble, TX 77338

Good News for Congregations

Gospel-energized resources from Concordia to help your church grow.

1. *Close the Back Door,* Alan F. Harre. 144 pp. Develops a ministry to inactives by providing a six-session course to train laity for visitation. 12-2867.

2. *Courageous Churches,* Paul T. Heinecke, Kent R. Hunter, David S. Luecke. 160 pp. Profiles how congregations put six principles for growth into practice. 12-3165.

3. *Evangelical Style and Lutheran Substance,* David Luecke. 128 pp. Helps churches develop new styles of ministry while maintaining the essential doctrinal substance. 12-3109.

4. *Evangelical Style and Lutheran Substance*—Study Guide, Har-

old Rau. 48 pp. Six-session course to help churches develop new styles while remaining faithful to their heritage. 20-2369.

5. *Everyone a Minister,* Oscar E. Feucht. 160 pp. A classic work on the priesthood of all believers. 12-2587.

6. *How to Manage Your Church,* Edgar Walz. 192 pp. A practical handbook for orienting new church leaders in the details of church administration. 12-3052.

7. *How to Develop a Team Ministry and Make It Work,* Ervin J. Henkelmann and Stephen J. Carter. 112 pp. A practical guide for building effective team ministry. 12-2879.

8. *Make Disciples,* Joel D. Heck. 112 pp. Detailed explanation and training in various methods of personal evangelism. 12-2869.

9. *Moving the Church into Action,* Kent R. Hunter. 152 pp. A creative contribution to help you develop the right mix of philosophy, goals, leadership, and style. 12-3135.

10. *New Designs for Church Leadership,* David Luecke. 176 pp. A comprehensive how-to guide for building leaders, followers, motivation, and full-bodied fellowship. 12-3148.

11. *New Member Assimilation,* Joel D. Heck. 112 pp. Provides a comprehensive program for assimilation, with descriptions of how seven churches are achieving it. 12-3110.

12. *Renewal for the 21st-Century Church,* Waldo J. Werning. 160 pp. Helps God's people take the first step in renewal: personal change. 12-3115.